EASY
CHARCUTERIE
BOARDS

EASY
CHARCUTERIE
BOARDS

ARRANGEMENTS, RECIPES, AND PAIRINGS FOR ANY OCCASION

MARCO NICCOLI & AUBREY NICCOLI

PHOTOGRAPHY BY ELYSA WEITALA

ROCKRIDGE
PRESS

For general information on our other products and services or to obtain technical support, please contact our Customer Care Department within the United States at (866) 744-2665, or outside the United States at (510) 253-0500.

Rockridge Press publishes its books in a variety of electronic and print formats. Some content that appears in print may not be available in electronic books, and vice versa.

Interior and Cover Designer: Liz Cosgrove, John Clifford
Art Producer: Samantha Ulban
Editor: Adrian Potts, Annie Choi
Production Editor: Andrew Yackira

Photography © 2021 Elysa Weitala. Food Styling by Victoria Woollard. Illustrations by Terry Marks, pp. 12–13. Cover: Three Kings' Day, page 46

ISBN: Print 978-1-64611-962-2
         eBook 978-1-64611-963-9
R0

FOR OUR FOUR CHILDREN,
NATALIA, HUDSON, LUNA, AND BRUNO,
WHO CONTINUALLY INSPIRE US TO REACH OUR DREAMS
AND BE THE BEST PARENTS WE CAN BE.
EVERYTHING WE DO IS FOR YOU.
LOVE, DAD AND MOM

CONTENTS

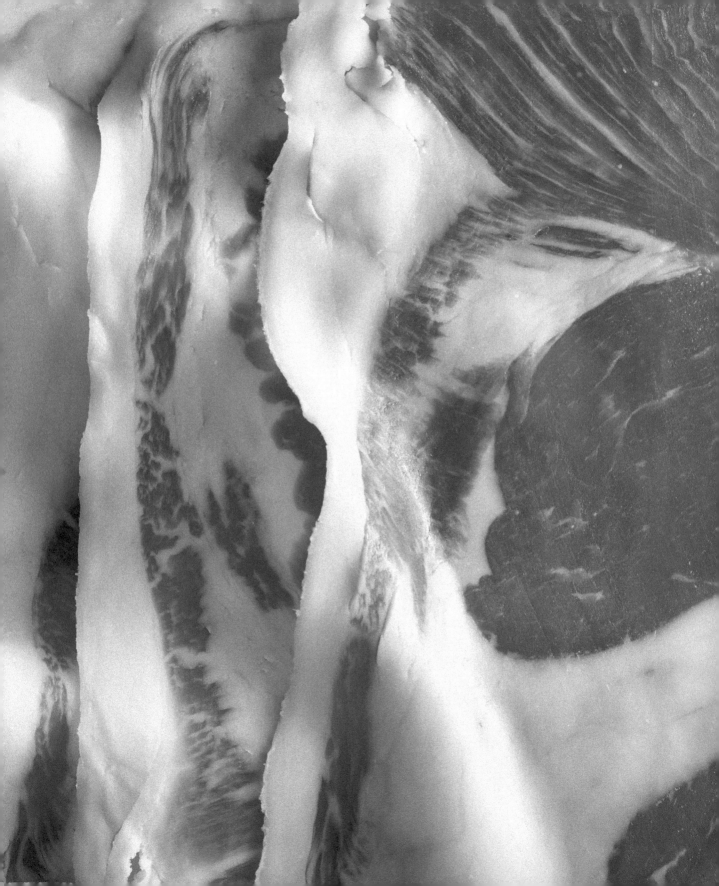

INTRODUCTION

AS TWO PROFESSIONAL CHEFS who both grew up in homes where cooking and family were quintessential, food has always been central to our lives. Before we married and founded our own culinary business, a m. niccoli (the initials of our names, Aubrey and Marco), we had each worked as a chef for years in the industry, taking our own paths through life and into the culinary world.

Fast-forward years later and through some life-changing events, we crossed paths and fell in love. As we were dating, we would show each other adoration the way chefs do—by cooking incredible meals or giving gifts of infused olive oils, beautifully flavored gelatos, interesting sweets, and other delicious foods. In fact, most of our relationship was built on having conversations while eating!

We have always believed in the power of bringing people together over a memorable meal. It's a tradition in our home to gather every Sunday with family and friends, and one of the most important offerings we produce is a beautiful charcuterie board. The ritual is a natural extension of our Italian and Spanish heritages, with parents and grandparents who taught us about ingredients and flavors common on antipasto and tapas plates.

Aside from being a great way to showcase and enjoy the incredible array of smoked, salted, and cured meats from the world of charcuterie, they are a perfect conversation starter and gathering place for guests. It has become so central to our get-togethers that we also include them in our chef business. When we prepare for events and celebrations, we always bring a charcuterie board to break the ice and get the conversation going. There is comfort and connection created when sharing thoughts and feelings over food.

Throughout this book we will show you how to make incredible charcuterie arrangements that will get your guests talking. There are 30 themed arrangements, ranging from small to large, for just about any occasion. We've also shared 32 of our recipes for accompaniments—such as dips, condiments, breads, pickles, jams, spreads, and other bites—to bring extra homemade flavors to your boards.

Our hope for the book is not just to walk you through the world of charcuterie and help you arrange a beautiful and delicious board, but to inspire you to forge even deeper connections with friends and family over a gorgeous spread. That is, after all, what the art of charcuterie is all about.

CHAPTER 1

THE ART OF CHARCUTERIE

CREATING A CHARCUTERIE BOARD is such a fun way to express yourself and be creative with food. By pairing quality ingredients with homemade items, you can showcase an amazing presentation your guests will love. We've shared a variety of our favorite arrangements throughout this book, with all kinds of boards themed by occasion or region and grouped according to the size of your event.

In this chapter, we will provide an overview of the different types of preserved meats that make up the world of charcuterie—roaming from Italy to Spain to France to Eastern Europe—before we dive into how to pair and arrange your boards in the next chapter.

WHAT IS CHARCUTERIE?

First things first: What do we mean when we say "charcuterie"? In its truest form, it refers to meat—usually pork—that has been preserved by salt-curing, smoking, air-curing, or brine-curing. It can also refer to a style of slow cooking in fat to make a confit.

While *charcuterie* is a French word, people across many cultures have been preserving meat for centuries. It was once a necessity to keep this precious commodity for a long period of time without spoiling, long before the invention of the refrigerator. This ancient style of preserving meats by drying and salting extended the life of meat during the heat of summer and kept it safe to eat over a long, cold winter.

In some regions, charcuterie includes preserving fish using similar methods, to produce delicacies such as smoked salmon, lox, and pickled herring.

In today's world, the term has come to mean pairing preserved meats or seafood with cheeses, fruits, and many other accompaniments to serve at gatherings and celebrations. During get-togethers in our own home, charcuterie spreads serve as a focal point for family and friends to socialize and enjoy an abundance of flavors and textures from all over the world.

TYPES OF CHARCUTERIE

While specialty meats and fish were once found only in artisanal stores in North America, a newfound interest in charcuterie has meant that supermarkets and local grocery stores are increasingly offering a greater variety of options that go well beyond old-school cold cuts.

These days you can find all manner of charcuterie, including both traditional varieties and more modern types with creative flavorings. Broadly speaking, though, charcuterie falls into a handful of categories related to the method of preservation.

SALT-CURED

The method of salt-curing meat is very simple—all it takes is salt, air, and time. Salt gradually draws moisture out of the meat, making it difficult for bacteria to survive and so producing a more shelf-stable product with a pleasingly salty flavor. This basic method of preservation is often combined with other forms, such as smoking, drying, and brining, to add flavor and texture.

Common types: bacon, lox, Parma ham, prosciutto

SMOKE-CURED

An ancient preservation method, smoke-curing involves exposing meat and fish to smoke, but without fully cooking it. It is commonly done by placing the food in an enclosed area over smoke produced at a low heat from smoldering wood or charcoal for a long period of time. This can also be done with cold smoke that cools when pulled into a separate chamber from where the product is held.

Smoke provides a coating on the surface of the product that prevents the growth of bacteria and also aids in dehydration, yielding tender and distinctly flavored foods. The depth of flavor can be further enhanced by changing the variety of wood. Apple and pecan woods are a couple of our favorites that add beautifully sweet notes.

Common types: smoked ham, smoked salmon, smoked sausages

AIR-CURED

Drying meat in gently circulating air is another popular method of preservation. The most commonly recognized air-cured meat is salami, which is flavored with aromatics such as pepper, garlic, and wine, then placed in casings to be hung in a temperature-controlled cellar for an extended period of time. Air-curing is also a key part of the cheese-making process.

Common types: biltong, jamón, jerky, salami

BRINE-CURED

Essentially an extension of basic salt-curing, this method of preservation involves submerging products in a brining solution of liquid and salt. The liquid can be water, beer, cider, fruit juice, or wine, flavored with aromatics such as pepper, citrus, herbs, and spices such as anise and cloves. This form of curing allows products to absorb extra seasoning while also preserving them with salt.

Common types: brined ham, brined pork belly, pastrami

CONFIT

Confit involves a combination of salt and animal fat. The meat is first dry-salted and then immersed in its own rendered fat at a low temperature for a long period of time. It is most commonly done with duck, and we even show you how to make your own for our South of France board (page 34). A life-changing variation is a confit rib eye clarified in tallow.

Common types: duck confit, goose confit, pork belly confit

FORCEMEAT

The softer side of charcuterie, forcemeats are pureed mixtures of meats, poultry, or fish combined with fats and seasoning to preserve and flavor the products. While these can be an acquired taste for some, the most common type on a charcuterie board is undoubtedly liver pâté, a rich, smooth delicacy that makes for a wonderful spread on a humble baguette. You can try it out on our Picnic in Paris board (page 18).

Common types: mousse, pâté, rillette, terrine

REGIONAL STYLES

While different cuisines around the globe have their own variations on preserving meat, the true home of charcuterie is

Europe, where it is a highly regional and seasonal affair, incorporating local ingredients at the peak of their freshness.

- **France:** The French are pioneers in charcuterie, where preserved meats are common in homes, restaurants, and wine bars across the country. They are masters of dry-curing to create delicacies such as jambon de Bayonne and saucisson sec, and experts in forcemeat products such as pâtés, mousses, and terrines.

- **Italy:** If you have ever been to Italy, you know it's common to see all kinds of small-batch salami hanging from the rafters in local shops and homes. They're just one type of an array of cured meats, known collectively as *salumi* and typically made from pork, to grace antipasto platters across the nation.

- **Spain:** Pork reigns supreme as the charcuterie item of choice on tapas plates in Spain. The most prized is jamón ibérico, which is artfully salt- and air-cured from heritage pigs. Also popular is chorizo, a cured or smoked pork sausage that is seasoned with garlic, paprika, and salt, among other variations.

- **Eastern Europe:** Often overlooked when it comes to charcuterie, Eastern Europe has its own traditions of salting and smoking meats. In Poland you can savor smoked or dried kielbasa, and in Hungary you'll find various types of salami and cured kolbász (sausage).

CHAPTER 2

ARRANGING YOUR BOARD

NOW THAT YOU KNOW a bit more about the history and varieties of charcuterie meats, it's time to turn our attention to the art of arranging a crowd-pleasing charcuterie board. A board is a blank canvas on which to mix and match a seemingly endless variety of tastes, textures, and colors, and that can seem a bit daunting at first. But by following the basic guidelines outlined in this chapter, it should become as easy and enjoyable as grazing on a finished arrangement with family and friends.

The first step in curating a great board is to know your audience. We use the same process when planning large events for clients as we do when planning a casual get-together with friends at home. Start with the guest count, so you know how many different items you'll need to provide and how much time you'll need to prepare. Take into account any dietary restrictions or allergies, and make sure there are suitable substitutes available.

Then it's time to consider the occasion and theme of the event, to inform the look and feel of your arrangement. For instance, is it a birthday, holiday, or date night? If it's a celebration, you will want an abundance of ingredients and colors. If it's a date night, you'll want something more low-key and refined.

The time of year can also influence your board. The season will help you decide what type of accompaniments and seasonal ingredients you'd like to use. Another option is to theme your board based on a country or region, selecting products from or inspired by a particular part of the world.

THE FIVE ELEMENTS OF A CHARCUTERIE BOARD

There are five key elements to building a charcuterie board. Make sure you have one or more items from each of these categories to create a balanced board with plenty of variety.

1. **Meat:** For a charcuterie lover, this will be the star of the show. It's worth it to splurge on high-quality meats. If you're catering to a larger group, choose two or more types.

2. **Cheese:** While there are hundreds of cheeses, a good basic rule is to choose two or more with different flavor profiles and textures. Choose one cow milk cheese, which can be soft or hard, and either a sheep or goat cheese, which are typically sharp and softer cheeses. That way you have something for everyone.

3. **Produce:** Fresh fruit like berries, grapes, and cherries look beautiful and bring balance to a plate. There is also all manner of dried, pickled, and brined items, such as gherkins and olives, to round things out. Nuts, such as pistachios, almonds, and hazelnuts, bring some welcome crunch.

4. **Dips and condiments:** These are finishing touches in terms of flavor profile and appearance. Your options include dips, jams, relishes, honey, mustards, and chutneys.

5. **Breads and crackers:** These are the platform on which to consume your charcuterie. They present a great opportunity to explore the specialty baked goods of regional cuisines and your local bakery. If you're preparing a spread for friends who can't eat gluten, then crackers made from rice, lentil, quinoa, and seeds are great choices.

PAIRING CHARCUTERIE WITH ACCOMPANIMENTS

Now comes the most creative part of the process: the art of the arrangement. Generally, you'll want to incorporate each of the five key elements of a board to create a harmony of colors, textures, and flavors.

THE LEAD ACTORS

First and foremost is to consider which charcuterie will take center stage. Once you know this, you can select the next most important component, the cheese. When the charcuterie and cheese are eaten together, consider how they will create balance and each enhance the flavor of the others. For example, if you've picked a rich and salty meat such as prosciutto or jamón, a creamy cheese like a nutty gruyère or milky mozzarella will provide equilibrium. If you've chosen a heavier, more seasoned meat like salami, go for a fresh and silky burrata or even a sharp cheddar as an interesting counterpoint.

THE SUPPORTING CAST

Once you have chosen the meat and cheese, the rest should start to fall into place. What fresh produce will brighten up the board and provide a contrast for the richness of the meats and cheeses? Dried fruits like apricots offer extra sweetness, and pickled foods like cornichons bring sweet and sour notes to round out the flavor profile. Brined items like olives offer a salty, tangy edge. And nuts are especially useful to include a contrasting texture on the board.

Dips and condiments help put the finishing touches on your board. Consider what flavor profile needs to be added. Need a light touch? Perhaps a ricotta or a hummus dip would work. Looking to bring extra acidity and bite? A tangy mustard can elevate the flavors of your meats and cheeses. Want a sweet or sour touch? Jams and preserves can offset salty and savory flavors.

BEHIND THE SCENES

You'll need some basic tools in your kitchen to bring together your charcuterie boards. Start with a cutting board. We prefer wood because it's easier on your knives. You'll need some kitchen knives for the cutting and slicing that goes on behind the scenes. You'll also need a tool for shaving harder cheeses. You can buy a fancy cheese shaver or just use a wide vegetable peeler.

We suggest a few small and medium bowls for mixing ingredients. You'll also need a kitchen scale to measure the ingredients listed in the boards in chapters 3, 4, and 5. Get a small, inexpensive digital scale. You should be able to find one online for under $20.

BRINGING IT ALL TOGETHER

Let's say your friends who are traveling to Paris soon are coming over for Sunday brunch. It's winter and you know you want to do a French theme. You could create a spread of jambon de Bayonne (or its Italian cousin, prosciutto), gruyère, croissants, freshly squeezed orange juice, espresso, sweet pastries, and marmalade.

Because it's winter, toasting the croissants with the meat and cheese stuffed inside couldn't be more warming. The chewy prosciutto, gooey melted cheese, and crisp toasted croissant offer an array of textures.

The delicate, salty flavor of the prosciutto pairs perfectly with gruyère, a sharp yet creamy cheese that melts well. Oranges are readily available in the winter, so freshly squeezing the juice is easy, and this sweet, tart, acidic touch serves as a palate cleanser. All of those flavors are sure to create a culinary experience. If you want to take it a step further, make your own Meyer Lemon Marmalade (page 94) for a balance of tart and sweet.

As you can see, on this board we have paired different flavors and textures. There is something salty, sweet, sour, and buttery, with a variety of savory notes, together with sweet and acidic tones to offset the savory. It's important to include all of them on each board.

DRINK PAIRINGS

With beverages as with food, flavor is always the key focus, but a secondary consideration is the theme of your celebration or reason for the event. Be sure to take a step back and think of your guests and their preferences so that you have something to offer everyone.

- **Wine:** A lighter meat is suited to a lighter wine, while richly seasoned charcuterie is better matched with a heartier wine. For a larger board with a wider variety, it is always nice to serve both red and white. If you would like to add another option, a rosé or sparkling wine can be a great option as well.

- **Beer:** Next on the list is a good-quality beer. Consider whether a light ale or a lager would be good to tame bold ingredients, or a fuller-bodied dark ale or IPA would enhance the richness and spice of your spread.

- **Cider:** A crisp and refreshing cider (with or without alcohol) is a great pairing for more summery and sweet arrangements.

- **Cocktails:** You can create a cocktail inspired by the theme of the board. This is where some fun and creativity can come into play.

- **Nonalcoholic drinks:** It's a nice touch and very courteous to have options for nondrinkers at your gathering. Any cocktail can become a mocktail with a little

HOW TO BUILD A BOARD

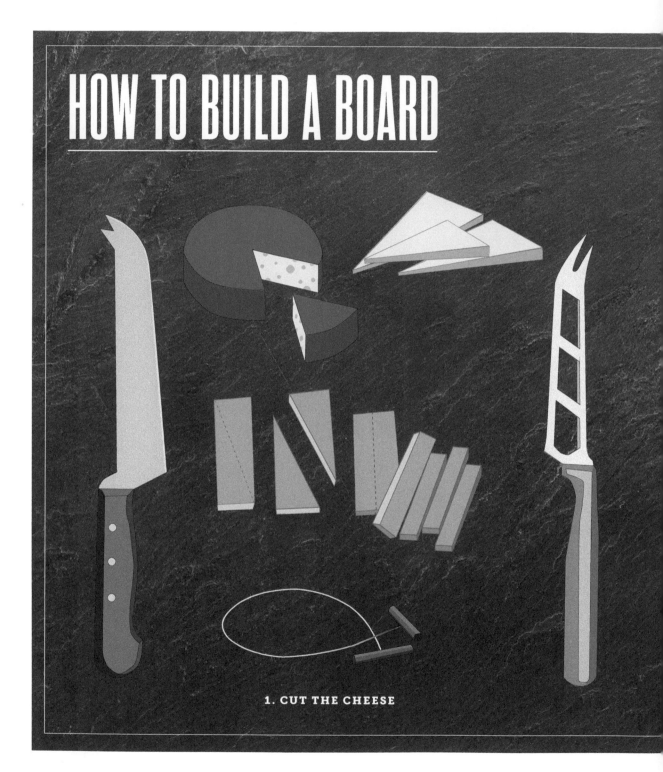

1. CUT THE CHEESE

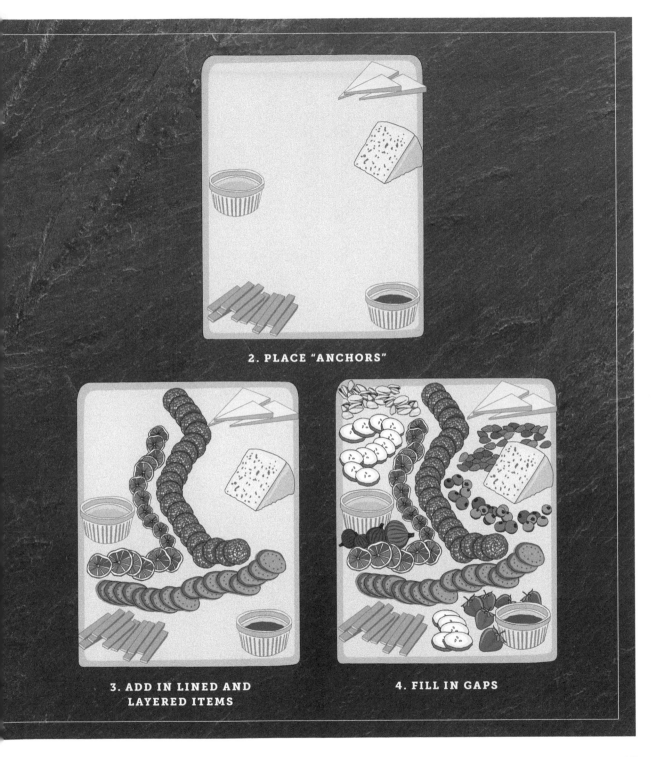

2. PLACE "ANCHORS"

3. ADD IN LINED AND
LAYERED ITEMS

4. FILL IN GAPS

substitution. Coffee, tea, and juices can also be a welcome addition for guests.

For each charcuterie arrangement in this book, we've suggested a drink pairing with some tasting notes. The important thing is to seek out the best quality of whatever you decide to offer.

MAKING IT BEAUTIFUL

When it comes to curating a picture-perfect board, achieving the right visual palette of your arrangement is just as important as pleasing the palates of your guests.

BOARDS, DISHES, AND UTENSILS

Sourcing a gorgeous board is very important, because it's the foundation of your presentation. You can build your charcuterie arrangement on marble, wood, ceramic, or stone. Wood and marble cutting boards are widely used and very beautiful. The bigger the statement the piece makes, the better.

Consider the size of the board or platter in relation to the number of people you are entertaining—a larger board for a big celebration or a small platter for an intimate get-together. You don't want a lot of ingredients getting crowded on a small board, or a few well-chosen items looking sparse and sad on a huge platter.

Matching small dishes for nuts, olives, dips and spreads are lovely—vary the sizes and heights to create variety. Typically, we recommend white dishes, which won't clash with any of the colors you choose for your meats, cheeses, and accompaniments. You might also find dishes that complement your individual board.

It is also very important—and elegant—to have a set of matching utensils

THE COLOR PALETTE

We eat first with our eyes—we're sure you've heard that many times. This is why it's important to be aware of color choices. Using a wide variety of hues instantly adds beauty to an arrangement. Carefully choosing and arranging the five key elements of the board will naturally bring contrast, but the vibrant colors of fresh fruit like berries, grapes, and vegetables will really make a board pop. You can also choose produce and accompaniments that are different shades of the same color for an interesting monochromatic look.

to accompany the cheeses and pairings. You'll need some small spoons, teaspoons, small serving forks, small spreading knives, small cutting knives, a small pair of tongs, and a few cheese knives (typically these are curved toward the tip and have two prongs at the end—the better to stick them into a wedge of cheese).

HOW TO USE THIS BOOK

This book includes 30 themed boards for any occasion, organized by size—you will find these in chapters 3, 4, and 5. We have listed all necessary serving pieces, ingredients, and instructions for assembling each of the arrangements, and offered a few pro tips to make things easier.

For boards that include recipes from chapters 6 and 7, you'll also find recipe prep times. Remember, though, that some accompaniments can be made in advance—we'll let you know which ones.

Some of the recipes, such as our duck confit, artisan focaccia, and oven-dried strawberries, may take a little longer to make, but you'll be rewarded with fresh and flavorful additions to your boards. Of course, if you find yourself short on time, you can always substitute store-bought alternatives. In fact, you need never feel constrained by time or ingredients; you can mix and match as you please with each board to choose your own charcuterie adventure.

As a handy reference tool, on page 97 you'll find a glossary of charcuterie meats with tasting notes, substitutions, and the boards they appear on in this book.

Happy arranging, eating and, entertaining!

Afternoon for Two, page 25

CHAPTER 3
SMALL BOARDS

PICNIC IN PARIS

SERVES 2

This charcuterie board is ideal for a quaint picnic for two. This grab-and-go list of ingredients can be packed in a basket and assembled on the beach, at the park, or after a short hike. Wrap the ingredients individually, or put them in separate containers. We love this board because all of the ingredients can be eaten separately or put together right onto the baguette to create a Parisian-inspired sandwich. The creamy brie and rich pâté serve as a perfect spread to build on. Adding a little whole-grain mustard for acidity and bite provides contrast for thinly sliced saucisson sec, a traditional French salami flavored with garlic and black pepper.

4 ounces saucisson sec, thinly sliced

2 pears

7 ounces double-cream brie

2 tablespoons whole-grain mustard

3 ounces pâté

1 baguette

You will need:
a basket or tote to carry your picnic, a small cutting board, a cutting knife, a spreading knife, 2 spoons, napkins, 2 wineglasses, a corkscrew

1. When you arrive at your destination, prepare the ingredients by thinly slicing the saucisson sec and arranging it on one corner of the board.

2. Core and slice the pears and place the slices on the opposite corner.

3. Add the brie almost in the center but offset toward another corner.

4. Add a spoonful of mustard next to the brie.

5. Place a small spoon in the pâté and place it near the pear slices.

6. Tear the baguette in half and stack it on or next to the board.

Drink pairing: La Mauriane, a French red wine flavored with black plum, blackberries, and wildflowers, is a beautiful pairing to complement the richness of the pâté and brie.

EUROPEAN BREAKFAST IN BED

SERVES 2

One of life's simplest and most satisfying indulgences is surely a cozy breakfast in bed. This board offers just that and needs very little prep. You can buy all of the items in advance so you're ready the morning of. Prosciutto and gruyère are a classic pairing of salty and nutty notes that are great melted together in a warm croissant. Artisan croissants from a local bakery are a nice added touch. A little pro tip is that they can be wrapped tightly in plastic wrap and frozen. When you are ready to use them, simply refresh them in the oven to bring back that flaky exterior and buttery aroma.

3 croissants

4 ounces gruyère (or Swiss cheese), thinly sliced

3 ounces prosciutto, thinly sliced

¼ cup citrus marmalade

1 tablespoon confectioners' sugar

You will need:
a platter big enough to serve two, a small bowl, a small spoon, a napkin

1. Preheat the oven to 375°F.

2. Place the croissants on a rimmed baking sheet and toast for 5 to 7 minutes.

3. Meanwhile, thinly slice the gruyère, then arrange the slices on one corner of the platter.

4. Separate the slices of prosciutto and place them on the platter next to one another.

5. Put the marmalade in a small bowl with a small spoon. Place it on the platter with a napkin under it so it doesn't slide.

6. Remove the croissants from the oven and place them directly on the center of the platter. Using a small, fine-mesh sieve, dust one with confectioners' sugar. Leave the other two as is.

Drink pairing: You can't go wrong with freshly squeezed orange juice to accompany this board. If you're in a mimosa type of mood, pour in some sparkling Italian prosecco. Finish up with a coffee or espresso to kick-start your day.

JAMÓN EXPERIENCE

SERVES 2

One of Spain's great gifts to gastronomy, legs of jamón ibérico can be seen hanging from the ceilings of the country's ubiquitous cured-ham shops. It's the star of many a tapas plate. In Barcelona, there's even a jamón museum where you can learn how it is cured and aged, and taste a slice carved right in front of you and placed on an oiled baguette. This board brings that tradition to your home, showcasing the delicate salty-sweet flavor of jamón ibérico along with Manchego, the country's rich and nutty semihard sheep milk cheese, made from sheep in the La Mancha wilderness in central Spain.

1 cup Castelvetrano olives (or any mild green olive), not pitted

6 ounces jamón ibérico (or prosciutto), thinly sliced

4 ounces Manchego (or any mild sheep milk cheese), broken into rough pieces

1 baguette

2 tablespoons garlic-infused olive oil

Sea salt

You will need:
a wooden board, a small bowl

1. Fill a small bowl with Castelvetrano olives and place it near the top right corner of the board.

2. Gently fold the jamón in wavy ribbons near the center top of the board.

3. Place the roughly broken pieces of Manchego below the jamón in the center of the board.

4. Tear the baguette in half. Leave one half intact, and with a serrated knife slice open the other half.

5. Gently brush a small amount of olive oil inside the sliced baguette pieces, then sprinkle the oiled sides with sea salt. Brush one stroke of oil across the top of the uncut piece. Place the bread on the left side of the board.

Drink pairing: Manzanilla is a Spanish sherry best served chilled to accompany cured meat or seafood. It has a dry, fresh, and delicate palate of floral notes reminiscent of chamomile, almonds, and yeast. It's absolutely perfect with jamón and this tapas-style spread.

KIDS IN BOLOGNA

SERVES 2

Are you looking for a playdate or after-school snack for the little ones in your life? Playtime and snack time come together in this board that allows kids to build their own combinations and eat with their hands, as kids love to do. The gentle flavors should please their young palates, too. And kids seem to love grissini, those long, thin, crispy Italian-style breadsticks. If you can't get your hands on some mortadella, you can use another deli meat your kids will enjoy.

6 grissini sticks

Small bundle fresh basil leaves

2 tablespoons balsamic reduction or glaze

1 cup cherry tomatoes

8 ounces fresh mozzarella bocconcini (or fresh mozzarella cut into bite-size pieces)

4 ounces mortadella (or any mild deli meat), thinly sliced

You will need: a small board, a tall glass, a mini bowl

1. Place the grissini in a glass sticking straight up and barely offset from the center of the board.

2. At the base of the grissini glass, place the bundle of basil and a mini bowl of balsamic reduction.

3. Visually divide the board in thirds (imagine drawing a peace sign on the board), and place the cherry tomatoes, bocconcini, and mortadella each in its own section.

Drink pairing: Chocolate egg cream—a delicious and kid-friendly blend of chocolate syrup, milk, and seltzer—is a classic of Italian American soda shops in New York City. For each serving, blend ½ cup whole milk and ¼ cup chocolate syrup together. If you have an immersion blender or high-speed blender, you can get that frothy texture and soda shop experience. Pour the chocolate milk into a tall glass and top with seltzer. Finish with a cute straw and serve. Pro tip: Chill the glasses in the freezer for a frosty cold treat.

SALAMI LOVERS WHO KETO

SERVES 2 / PREP TIME: 45 MINUTES

Who says charcuterie and dieting can't go hand in hand? Not only will this board please salami lovers, it doubles as the perfect artisanal fix for anybody on a low-carb keto-genic diet. The salami and black pepper bring some kick, and are nicely complemented by the creamy garlic ricotta and crispy chaffles—a low-carb take on waffles made of cheese and eggs that serve as a great base for the ingredients. The ratio of fat to protein (in grams) on this low-carb board is almost 50-50, making it a guilt-free spread for any keto followers.

1 cup fresh garlic ricotta (page 90, see Variation)

4 Mini Chaffles (page 72)

Extra-virgin olive oil, for drizzling

Freshly ground black pepper

3 ounces salami picante, casing removed, thinly sliced

3 ounces Creminelli Whiskey Salami Minis (or any mild salami)

You will need: a board, a small bowl, a small spoon, a small upright dish or glass

1. Prepare the fresh garlic ricotta and chaffles according to the recipes. The ricotta can be prepared up to a week ahead of time, but the chaffles are best served warm or at room temperature.

2. Place the ricotta in a small bowl with a spoon, near the center of the board but slightly to the left. Drizzle it with olive oil and grind some pepper over the top.

3. Arrange the chaffles off to the right side of the ricotta, stacking and shingling them to look pretty.

4. Arrange the salami slices below the ricotta.

5. Put the mini salami sticks in a small upright dish or glass near the top left side of the board.

Drink pairing: Keeping with the keto theme, pair this spread with some replenishing electrolyte water. Packed with sodium, potassium, and magnesium, this is a must for keto dieters (who tend to lose electrolytes due to water loss) and a great pick-me-up for anybody who wants to feel hydrated and refreshed. In a pitcher, combine 3 cups filtered water, ¼ teaspoon sea salt, 130 mg potassium powder, and 45 mg magnesium powder. Squeeze in the juice of half a lemon and stir well to mix.

SUMMER BERRY FIELDS

SERVES 2 / PREP TIME: 3 HOURS

This bright and beautiful spread can be made for brunch with a loved one or as a post-dinner dessert. If you haven't tried oven-dried strawberries yet, your life is about to be changed. It's the highlight of this board and a delicious natural treat. They take a long time to prepare, but you can make a big batch and store them for 2 weeks. Some lightly sautéed pancetta brings a crisp charcuterie element to the board, pairing nicely with the mascarpone, brioche, and honey.

1 cup Oven-Dried Strawberries (page 62)

4 ounces pancetta, thinly sliced

1 tablespoon olive oil

1 tablespoon granulated sugar

2 teaspoons lemon juice

½ cup blackberries

1 cup raspberries

4 thick slices brioche

2 tablespoons unsalted butter

Pinch ground cinnamon

Pinch confectioners' sugar

8 ounces mascarpone cheese

2 tablespoons honey

You will need:
a platter, a small bowl, a small spoon, a butter knife, a small jar, a honey wand

1. Prepare the oven-dried strawberries according to the recipe. The strawberries can be prepared up to 2 weeks ahead of time.

2. Heat a skillet over high heat. Add the pancetta and drizzle with the olive oil. Sauté the pancetta for 6 to 8 minutes, until it crisps up like cooked bacon. Set aside.

3. In a medium bowl, mix together the granulated sugar and lemon juice. Add the blackberries and raspberries, and gently toss to coat them with the mixture. Set aside to steep for 5 minutes.

4. Toast the brioche slices and spread with the butter. Place the brioche along the left side of the board, from the top to just below the center. Top the brioche with the macerated raspberries and blackberries. Finish with a sprinkling of cinnamon and confectioners' sugar.

5. Spoon the mascarpone into a heap near the lower right corner of the brioche.

6. Place the crispy pancetta on the top right corner of the board.

7. Pile the oven-dried strawberries in a small bowl, and place it in the bottom left corner with a small serving spoon next to it.

8. Just above or next to the strawberries, place the honey in a small jar with a honey wand.

Drink pairing: A French champagne is a great accompaniment to this board. If you are celebrating and want to splurge, Dom Pérignon is the ultimate pairing, but if you'd like to go with something lower-key but still elegant, fresh, and light, an authentic Brut such as Canard-Duchêne is great, too.

CHERRIES AND ALMONDS

SERVES 2 / PREP TIME: 45 MINUTES

This board screams summer. It's best enjoyed when all varieties of cherries come to the farmers' market. The robust flavor of bresaola, a dry-cured beef from Italy, complements the cherries flawlessly. Honeycomb is the natural wax structure made by bees, with raw honey inside its cells. You can eat the wax along with the honey or run a knife over it to push the honey out of the cells. Add the crunch of pecan granola and you are on your way to a most satisfying brunch, lunch, snack, midday date, or get-together with a friend.

½ cup Pecan Granola (page 88)

2 cups plain Greek yogurt

4 ounces bresaola (or lonzino), thinly sliced

2 cups cherries

1 cup Marcona almonds (or any salted blanched almonds)

5 to 6 ounces honeycomb squares

You will need: a board, 2 small bowls, 2 spoons, a small knife

1. Prepare the pecan granola according to the recipe. The granola can be prepared up to a month ahead of time.

2. Divide the Greek yogurt into two small bowls and top each with half of the pecan granola. Set the bowls side by side in the center of a large board with a spoon in each bowl.

3. In the top right corner, arrange the bresaola.

4. In the bottom left corner, add the cherries.

5. Above the cherries, pile the Marcona almonds.

6. On the bottom right, add the honeycomb squares, with a small knife.

Drink pairing: The sweetness and textures of this board make an exciting pairing with kriek, a hoppy, cherry-flavored beer from Belgium typically made with sour cherries. American brewery Strange Craft Beer Company makes a great one, but for the real deal, try Belgium's Lindemans Brewery kriek lambic beer.

AFTERNOON FOR TWO

SERVES 2 / PREP TIME: 50 MINUTES

The starring charcuterie of this casual, Italian-inspired arrangement is Barolo salami, which is traditionally cured in wine from the Piedmont region. It pairs perfectly with burrata, a luxurious fresh cheese with a silky, creamy texture, and our homemade pancetta-onion jam and cabernet balsamic reduction. The arugula adds a peppery fresh bite, and you can soak up all the flavors with an artisanal fougasse—a flattish bread that's shaped to resemble an ear of wheat.

¼ cup Pancetta-Onion Jam (page 92)

2 tablespoons Cabernet Balsamic Reduction (page 80)

8 ounces burrata (or fresh mozzarella)

1 cup arugula

Sea salt

Freshly ground black pepper

Extra-virgin olive oil

4 ounces Barolo salami (or any richly seasoned salami), thinly sliced

2 small loaves fougasse (or focaccia or ciabatta)

You will need: a board, a cheese knife, a small bowl, a small spoon

1. Prepare the pancetta-onion jam and cabernet balsamic reduction according to the recipes. The jam can be prepared up to 2 weeks ahead of time, and the reduction up to 3 months ahead of time.

2. Place the burrata in the center of a small board and top with the arugula, letting it naturally cascade around the cheese. Season with salt, pepper, and a drizzle of olive oil. Place the cheese knife next to the burrata.

3. Spoon the pancetta jam in the bottom left corner, near the base of the burrata.

4. Pour the cabernet balsamic reduction into a small bowl and place it in the right top corner with a small spoon in it.

5. Add the salami near the balsamic reduction in the right corner.

6. Cut the bread into small pieces and scatter them in the bottom right corner.

Drink pairing: Cabernet Sauvignon is a scrumptious and fruity full-bodied red wine that is a beautiful complement to the complex flavors of the Barolo salami, pancetta-onion jam, and balsamic reduction. Simply choose your favorite bottle and you cannot go wrong.

Spring in Valencia, page 30

CHAPTER 4
MEDIUM BOARDS

EVERYTHING BRUNCH

SERVES 4 / PREP TIME: 30 MINUTES

This board is great for hosting a small weekend brunch with friends. The charcuterie element comes in the form of smoked salmon, a method of preserving fish with origins stretching back as far as ancient Greece. The other star of this platter is the homemade everything lavash, with a flavor combo inspired by everything bagels (although you could use actual bagels instead, in a pinch). You can prepare them ahead of time, or even the day before.

1 Everything Lavash (page 77)

12 ounces smoked salmon, sliced

1 cup cream cheese

1 bunch fresh dill, torn into small pieces

1 bunch fresh chives, minced

6 vine-ripened Campari tomatoes (or grape tomatoes)

1 (3.5-ounce) jar capers, drained

1 red onion, thinly sliced

You will need:

a large platter or board, a medium bowl, 2 small bowls, 2 small spoons, a spreading knife, small serving tongs

1. Prepare the lavash according to the recipe, and cut into 8 pieces. The lavash can be prepared up to 4 days ahead of time.

2. Fill a medium bowl with the lavash, standing them upright to create height. Place the bowl in the top left corner of the board, with any pieces that didn't fit in the bowl under it.

3. In the bottom right corner, arrange the smoked salmon slices, overlapping them slightly to give them some volume.

4. Fill a small bowl with cream cheese and place it in the bottom left corner. Place the spreading knife in the cream cheese with the handle sticking up. Garnish the cream cheese with some of the dill and chives. Place the remaining dill next to the right of the bowl, closing the gap between the cream cheese and salmon.

5. Place the tomatoes with the vines still intact in the top right corner of the board.

6. Put the capers in a small bowl with a small spoon, and place that next to the tomatoes.

7. Loosely arrange the onion slices under the tomatoes and between the salmon.

Drink pairing: Grapefruit mimosas make a great sweet-tart pairing for this brunch. Simply combine one part fresh grapefruit juice with three parts chilled champagne (or ginger ale for a virgin mimosa). To garnish the rim of the glasses, combine your favorite smoked salt with grated lemon zest in a shallow dish, rub the rim of the glass with a lemon wedge, and dip into the salt mixture.

Preparation tip: You can do most of the arranging and prep for this board the night before. Simply leave off the lavash (store that in a zip-top bag in your pantry), cover the whole board with plastic wrap, and refrigerate. The morning of, simply add the lavash to the board and you are ready to entertain.

HIGH TEA

This arrangement makes a charming tea party, whether it's for a birthday party, bridal or baby shower, or even just a quaint lunch with friends. The cranberry Wensleydale has a clean, mild flavor profile with a slightly sweet honey undertone that pairs especially well with the classic brined and smoked soft ham. A little piece of mild, salty, and crumbly Cheshire cheese is heavenly on our thyme shortbread crackers. And it wouldn't be a true tea party without miniature cucumber sandwiches.

12 piece Thyme Shortbread (page 73)

½ cup cream cheese

8 slices white bread

1 English cucumber, thinly sliced

5½ ounces cranberry Wensleydale cheese (or fruit-infused stilton)

7 ounces Cheshire cheese (or mild cheddar)

4 ounces country ham, thinly sliced

1 bunch green grapes

You will need:
a medium platter,
2 cheese knives

1. Prepare the thyme shortbread according to the recipe. The shortbread can be prepared up to a week ahead of time.

2. Make the cucumber sandwiches by spreading the cream cheese evenly on 4 slices of bread. Shingle thin slices of cucumber over the cream cheese. Top each sandwich with another slice of bread. Cut off the crusts, then cut each sandwich diagonally into quarters and set aside.

3. Arrange the cranberry Wensleydale on the top left corner of the platter. Crumble a few pieces off one corner and leave a cheese knife sticking out of the top.

4. Add the Cheshire in the bottom right corner, with a cheese knife beside it.

5. Loosely arrange the ham slices just above the Cheshire, filling the top right area.

6. Shingle the thyme shortbread cookies in the bottom left corner of the board.

7. Place a heaping pile of green grapes in the center of the board, letting the bunches touch the edges of the cheeses and ham.

8. Stack and arrange the cucumber sandwiches in the middle left side of the board.

Drink pairings: While you can opt for a classic Earl Grey or English breakfast tea with a splash of milk if you wish to stick with tradition, a variety of herbal and green teas will bring some lighter refreshment. Cranberry hibiscus, rooibos, chamomile, and peppermint green tea are some favorites. If possible, provide adorable teacups and saucers.

SPRING IN VALENCIA

SERVES 4 / PREP TIME: 20 MINUTES, PLUS 3 HOURS TO CHILL

Inspired by the produce and flavors of the Spanish region of Valencia, this vibrant board is perfect for hosting a small lunch. Spain's famed charcuterie, jamón, makes an appearance, alongside another Mediterranean favorite, bresaola, which is made from beef that has been salted and dry-cured. It has a beautiful red color and pairs beautifully with the dark cherries. The salty, rich, smooth jamón makes a lovely accompaniment to the sweet and spicy apricot-chipotle gummies.

32 Apricot-Chipotle
Gummies (page 65)

8 ounces Manchego
(or any semihard sheep
milk cheese)

4 fresh apricots

6 ounces bresaola
(or lonzino)

6 ounces jamón,
thinly sliced

1½ cups Bing cherries
(or any variety)

You will need: a
medium board, a small
bowl, a cheese knife,
2 (4-by-4-inch) parchment paper squares, a
small knife

1. Prepare the apricot-chipotle gummies according to the recipe. The gummies can be prepared up to 2 weeks ahead of time.

2. Thinly slice about a third of the Manchego, creating a lacy look. Place the rest of the wedge near the center of the board but offset to the upper left. Put the slices next to the wedge and place a knife so it's sticking out of the top of the wedge.

3. Cut 2 apricots in half, exposing the stones. Cut the other 2 in quarters, discard their stones, and arrange together in the bottom left corner of the board.

4. Thinly slice half of the bresaola and place the remaining piece with the slices in the middle to bottom right area of the board, with a small knife.

5. Loosely arrange the jamón slices in the top right corner.

6. Fill a small bowl with the cherries and place it near the center of the board. Scatter a few cherries around the sides of the bowl to give an overflowing look.

7. To the left of the Manchego, place the two pieces of parchment paper overlapping each other, tucking an edge under the Manchego wedge. Arrange the gummies on the paper, loosely stacking them.

Drink pairing: Apricot sour cocktails make a spirited accompaniment to this board, providing that perfect pucker with a subtle effervescence. To make one, combine 2 ounces apricot brandy, 2 ounces sour mix, and ½ ounce simple syrup in a shaker with ice. Strain over a cocktail glass filled with ice, and finish with a splash of club soda and a slice of fresh apricot.

ROMAN WINTER

The bold flavors of brined pastrami and prosciutto cotto (cooked ham) plus the accompanying cheeses make for a hearty combo during the cold winter months. The cured meat is paired with sharp, salty pecorino romano and smooth, creamy mozzarella. The homemade cabernet balsamic reduction helps tie all the flavors and textures together. If you don't manage to make the recipe, store-bought balsamic glaze will suffice. Serve with homemade focaccia, olive oil, and fresh basil, and you have yourself a Roman holiday at home.

1 cup Cabernet Balsamic Reduction (page 80)

1 Artisan Focaccia (page 74)

6 ounces pastrami, thinly sliced

6 ounces prosciutto cotto (or country ham), thinly sliced

8 ounces fresh mozzarella

8 ounces pecorino romano (or Parmesan)

1 bunch fresh basil

Extra-virgin olive oil, for drizzling

You will need: a large board, a 4-ounce glass jar with an attached lid, 2 cheese knives (1 pronged)

1. Prepare the cabernet balsamic reduction and focaccia according to the recipes. The reduction can be prepared up to 3 months ahead of time, but the focaccia is best served warm or at room temperature.

2. Arrange the pastrami and prosciutto cotto in the center of the board, keeping each variety separate.

3. Place the fresh mozzarella in the top right corner and the wedge of pecorino romano in the bottom left corner. Stick a pronged cheese knife into the pecorino and the other cheese knife near the mozzarella.

4. Tuck the bundle of basil next to the mozzarella.

5. Add the jar of balsamic reduction in the top right area, near the mozzarella.

6. Cut or tear the focaccia into large chunks, and place them around the top left corner.

7. Place a bottle of olive oil next to the board for drizzling.

Drink pairing: Birra Moretti is a golden and slightly bitter Italian beer that makes a great match for this board. Serve it chilled in frosty glasses. If you can't find this brand, choose your favorite craft beer.

Serving suggestion: This board is a great opportunity to host a casual lunch with friends, with the option to make sandwiches from the ingredients. Or it could even be a quick weekday dinner at home. There is something so homey and intimate when building and eating with your hands, customizing each bite.

HUNTING IN MANCHESTER

SERVES 4 / PREP TIME: 1 HOUR 15 MINUTES, PLUS 3 HOURS TO CHILL

This board is tailor-made for lovers of game meats. You can find wild boar salami (we like Creminelli brand) and duck jerky (we like Mountain America, which is hickory-smoked and rubbed with black pepper). The drunken goat cheese is from the Murcia region of Spain. It has a wine scent and a mildly fruity flavor, and makes a crumbly, tart addition to brighten up the board. The Yorkshire puddings—a favorite recipe in our family for years—are a nostalgic British staple typically served with a roast dinner. Here, these eggy, airy little rolls are the ideal vessel to dive into the creamy caramelized onion dip.

1 cup Caramelized Onion Dip (page 93)

8 Yorkshire Puddings (page 76)

5½ ounces wild boar salami (or any bold-flavored salami)

1 bundle chives, finely chopped

6 ounces drunken goat cheese (or sweet goat cheese)

6½ ounces duck jerky (or turkey jerky), cut into thin pieces

You will need:
a medium board, a small bowl, a small spoon, a cheese knife, a small knife

1. Prepare the caramelized onion dip and Yorkshire puddings according to the recipes. The dip can be prepared up to a month ahead of time, but the Yorkshire puddings are best made immediately before arranging the board.

2. Remove the casing from the wild boar salami and thinly slice about half. Place the slices and the remaining large piece near the bottom left quadrant of the board, with a small knife.

3. In the top left corner, add the bowl of onion dip, garnish with the chives, and place a small spoon next to the bowl.

4. To the right of the onion dip, place all of the Yorkshire puddings, filling the space around the bowl.

5. Place the goat cheese in the lower right corner of the board and slightly crumble off about 2 inches from one end. Then stick a cheese knife into the rest of the cheese.

6. Pile the jerky pieces next to the cheese in an open space.

Drink pairings: We recommend pairing High West Campfire Whiskey with this board. It's a very distinctive blend of bourbon, scotch, and rye whiskey that makes for an intriguing accompaniment. For a nonalcoholic beverage, we suggest a craft soft cider.

SWEET BELGIUM

SERVES 4 / PREP TIME: 10 MINUTES

The ultimate spread for anybody with a sweet tooth, this festive dessert board is perfect for Valentine's Day, a double date, movie night, or just a special treat with friends. It features a playful twist on charcuterie: chocolate salami. A popular dessert across Europe, it resembles traditional salami visually, but forgoes meat for cocoa, broken biscuits, butter, eggs, and a bit of port wine or rum. Elsewhere there are croissants and fromage de Bruxelles, a spreadable cow milk cheese with strong citrusy and salty notes. The finishing touch is our homemade date caramel spread, which has the sweetness and texture of caramel but no added sugar.

1 cup Date Caramel (page 89)

5½ ounces chocolate salami (or dark chocolate)

5 ounces fromage de Bruxelles (or any soft cow milk cheese, or double-cream brie)

4 hazelnut croissants (or plain croissants spread with Nutella)

4 plain croissants

1 cup raspberries

2 cups strawberries

You will need: a large board, a small knife, a small bowl, a small spoon, a cheese knife

1. Prepare the date caramel spread according to the recipe. If necessary, this can be made up to 3 days ahead of time, but it's best served fresh.

2. Slice half of the chocolate salami into thin rounds. Place the slices and the remaining large piece in the bottom right corner of the board. Put a small knife next to it.

3. In the center of the board, place the fromage de Bruxelles with a cheese knife.

4. Put the date caramel spread in a small bowl with a spoon and place it in the top right corner of the board with a small spoon in the bowl.

5. Stack the croissants along the left side of the board.

6. Scatter the raspberries on the fromage, cascading down one side.

7. Fill in the blank spaces around the date caramel bowl with the strawberries.

Drink pairing: An espresso martini is an invigorating drink to accompany this board. To make one, combine 2 ounces vodka (we like White Nights Vodka from Belgium), ½ ounce simple syrup, ½ ounce coffee liqueur, and 1 ounce chilled brewed espresso in a cocktail shaker filled with ice. Shake well, then strain into a martini glass garnished with a rim of chocolate sprinkles.

SOUTH OF FRANCE

SERVES 4 / PREP TIME: 2 HOURS 25 MINUTES

This elegant board showcases duck confit, a form of charcuterie hailing from the southwestern French region of Gascony. The complexity and richness of this delicacy complements the simplicity of fromage blanc, a soft, creamy cow milk cheese with hints of nuttiness. It can be flavored by adding roasted garlic or grated citrus zest and honey to sweeten it up, if you'd like. The homemade mustard gastrique brings a sharp, tangy contrast to tie the trio together. Black pepper crackers make a great base—we like La Panzanella Black Pepper Croccantini. Taking this board over the top is the classic trio of caviar, hard-boiled egg, and onion.

12 ounces Duck Confit (page 71)

½ cup Mustard Gastrique (page 83)

8 ounces fromage blanc (or quark)

2 ounces caviar

4 large hard-boiled eggs, diced small

1 small red onion, minced

6 ounces black pepper crackers

You will need: a large platter, 2 small bowls, a small serving fork, 2 small spoons, a small dish, a caviar spoon, 4 small teaspoons

1. Prepare the duck confit and mustard gastrique according to the recipes. The confit can be prepared up to 3 months ahead of time and reheated, and the gastrique can be prepared up to 2 weeks ahead of time and reheated.

2. Put the warm duck confit in a small bowl with a serving fork, and place the bowl on the top left side of the board.

3. Place the fromage blanc in a small bowl with a spoon on the bottom right side of the board.

4. Place the caviar in a small bowl in the center of the board, with the caviar spoon in it. Place the teaspoons beside it.

5. To the left of the caviar, place the diced hard-boiled eggs. Just above the eggs, place the minced red onion.

6. Below the caviar, spoon the warm mustard gastrique directly onto the board, then use the back of the spoon to pull it to the right, creating an artful look. Leave the spoon to the side.

7. Arrange the crackers in both the upper right and lower left quadrants.

Drink pairing: A delicate and fruity champagne will provide a crisp, refreshing contrast to the flavors of this board. We recommend Le Mesnil Blanc de Blancs Grand Cru, which has a subtle fruitiness perfumed with hints of apple and pear and is readily available online.

Ingredient tip: You can use whatever kind of caviar appeals to you. Unopened caviar can be stored in the refrigerator for about 2 weeks.

THE SICILIAN TABLE

SERVES 4 / PREP TIME: 1 HOUR 10 MINUTES, PLUS 1 HOUR TO BRINE OLIVES,
AND OVERNIGHT TO FERMENT FOCACCIA

This spread is inspired by the flavors of Sicily, where olive and pistachio trees grow wild throughout the countryside. If you can, use Sicilian pistachios, which are stronger and sharper in flavor than other varieties. Sicilian pistachios have been used as an ingredient in salami-making on the island for centuries, bringing a wonderful nuttiness and texture to balance the salt and fat of the meat. You can buy this salami with pistachios online, or simply use any good-quality salami, slice it, and dust the slices with chopped salted pistachios. Its sister charcuterie on this board is fennel salami (finocchiona), which is richly flavored with fennel seeds and seasonings.

2 cups Rosemary-Lemon
Castelvetrano Olives
(page 64)

1 Artisan Focaccia
(page 74), cut into
large squares

1 (4-ounce) log
goat cheese

¼ cup chopped
salted pistachios

5½ ounces salami
with pistachios (or any
flavorful salami), sliced

5½ ounces fennel salami
(or any herb-infused
salami), sliced

You will need: a
large board, a small
cheese knife, a medium
bowl, a spoon

1. Prepare the rosemary-lemon olives and artisan focaccia according to the recipes. The olives can be prepared up to a week ahead of time, but the focaccia is best served warm or at room temperature.

2. Roll the log of goat cheese in the chopped pistachios. Place the log to the left center of the board. Stick a small cheese knife in the top of it.

3. Place the pistachio salami slices in the left bottom corner of the board.

4. Place the fennel salami in the bottom right corner of the board.

5. Fill a medium bowl with the marinated olives, add a spoon, and place it in the top right area of the board.

6. Scatter the focaccia squares along the top of the board, reaching from side to side.

Drink pairing: Keeping with the theme, you can pair this board with an olive vermouth, the sister to the well-known dirty martini. It's a briny cocktail that will complement the citrus notes of the olives and saltiness of the salami. In a tumbler, combine ⅔ ounce dry vermouth, ⅓ ounce fresh orange juice, 1 ounce scotch whiskey, and a few ice cubes. Stir well for about 20 seconds. Strain into a cocktail glass and finish with 3 Castelvetrano olives on a stick. A mocktail version can be made with white grape juice in place of the vermouth and a splash of cream soda in place of the scotch.

HAPPY HOUR TAPAS

SERVES 4 / PREP TIME: 50 MINUTES

This board pays homage to tapas, Spain's famously delicious version of appetizers. You'll typically encounter various types of charcuterie, cheese, seafood, olives, and the very traditional potato omelet (called a tortilla) in most establishments. Here we've showcased Spanish chorizo, a spicy cured pork sausage flavored with garlic and paprika, which is nicely matched with Manchego marinated in chili oil. The spread also features the milder salchichón ibérico, a dry-cured hard salami flavored with sea salt and black pepper. The crushed tomato crostini cools down all the powerful flavors and brings a bright ending to the proceedings.

For the chili oil Manchego

12 ounces Manchego (or any mild sheep milk cheese), cut into bite-size pieces

1 fresh chile, thinly sliced

1 cup extra-virgin olive oil

For the crushed tomato crostini

1 baguette, sliced

1 garlic clove, cut in half

Extra-virgin olive oil, for drizzling

1 large, ripe heirloom tomato

To make the chili oil Manchego

1. Put the Manchego pieces in a medium jar. Add the chile slices and pour in the olive oil, making sure the cheese is submerged.

2. Screw on the lid and set aside for at least 1 hour so the oil and peppers can infuse fully into the cheese.

To make the crushed tomato crostini

3. Preheat the oven to 375°F.

4. Spread out the baguette slices on a rimmed baking sheet. Toast in the oven for 7 minutes.

5. Rub one side of each slice with a cut garlic clove and drizzle with olive oil.

6. In a food processor or blender, pulse the tomato until it resembles a coarse salsa.

To make the board

7. Prepare the Spanish tortilla according to the recipe. The tortilla can be prepared the day before and reheated. Cut it into 1-by-2-inch rectangles and place the pieces in the center of the board. Top with the arugula, a drizzle of olive oil, and a few grinds of black pepper.

For the board

½ **Spanish Tortilla (page 70)**

1 **cup arugula**

Extra-virgin olive oil, for drizzling

Freshly ground black pepper

Sea salt

6 **ounces salchichón ibérico (or any Spanish hard salami), sliced**

6 **ounces chorizo, sliced**

You will need:

a medium board, a jar with a cover, a small fork

8. Place the crostini along the bottom of the board, from the center to the right side. Spoon the tomato puree over the crostini and season with sea salt and freshly ground black pepper.

9. Place the salchichón ibérico slices in the top right area of the board.

10. Place the chorizo slices in the bottom left corner of the board.

11. Put a small fork in the jar of Manchego and place it in the top left.

Drink pairing: A young or aged Tempranillo, a full-bodied Spanish red wine, would be a great choice for this board. Depending on your preference, you could also go with a young, fruitier version or an aged, bold, high-tannin wine with hints of cherry, fig, and cedar.

SOUR THEN SWEET

SERVES 4 / PREP TIME: 25 MINUTES, PLUS 25 MINUTES TO BRINE

The varied ingredients on this board may seem like a strange combination at first, but together they create a surprising balance of textures and sweet and sour tastes. The brined cucumber ribbons are delicious on top of the pickled herring—a deliciously sweet and sour brined fish that is popular throughout northern Europe—alongside creamy mascarpone cheese spread over the sourdough baguette. A piece of SeaHive cheddar (made in Utah from Jersey cow milk, honey, and salt) stacked on a slice of tart Granny Smith apple with a drizzle of sweet honey and candied nuts is sensational.

4 cups Brined Cucumber Ribbons (page 60)

2 cups Spiced Candied Nuts (page 87)

8 ounces SeaHive cheddar (or any mild white cheddar)

8 ounces pickled herring

8 ounces mascarpone

¼ cup honey

2 Granny Smith apples, cored and sliced

1 sourdough baguette

You will need:
a large board, a small cheese knife, a pint-size canning jar, 2 small cocktail forks, a small dish, a small bowl, a small spreading knife or spoon, a small honey jar, a honey wand

1. Prepare the brined cucumber ribbons and spiced candied nuts according to the recipes. The cucumbers can be prepared up to a week ahead of time and the nuts up to 3 months.

2. Place the cheddar in the bottom right corner of the board with a small cheese knife next to it.

3. Place the brined cucumber ribbons in a pint-size jar below the top left corner. Add a small cocktail fork to the jar.

4. Put the pickled herring into a small dish with a cocktail fork, and place it next to the cucumber ribbons but slightly offset.

5. In the top center of the board, place the mascarpone in a bowl with a small spreading knife or spoon.

6. Put the honey in a small jar with a honey wand, and place it to the right of the mascarpone.

7. Sprinkle the candied nuts near the cheddar in the bottom center of the board.

8. Place the Granny Smith slices in the center of the board.

9. Tear the baguette into large pieces and place them along the top right side of the board near the herring.

Drink pairing: A green appletini is the perfect sour and sweet drink to accompany this arrangement. In a cocktail shaker, combine 1 ounce Smirnoff Green Apple Vodka, ½ ounce sour mix, 3 ounces apple cider, and some ice cubes. Shake well, then strain into a cocktail glass and coat the rim with a 1-to-2 salt-to-sugar ratio. Garnish with a small wedge of Granny Smith apple.

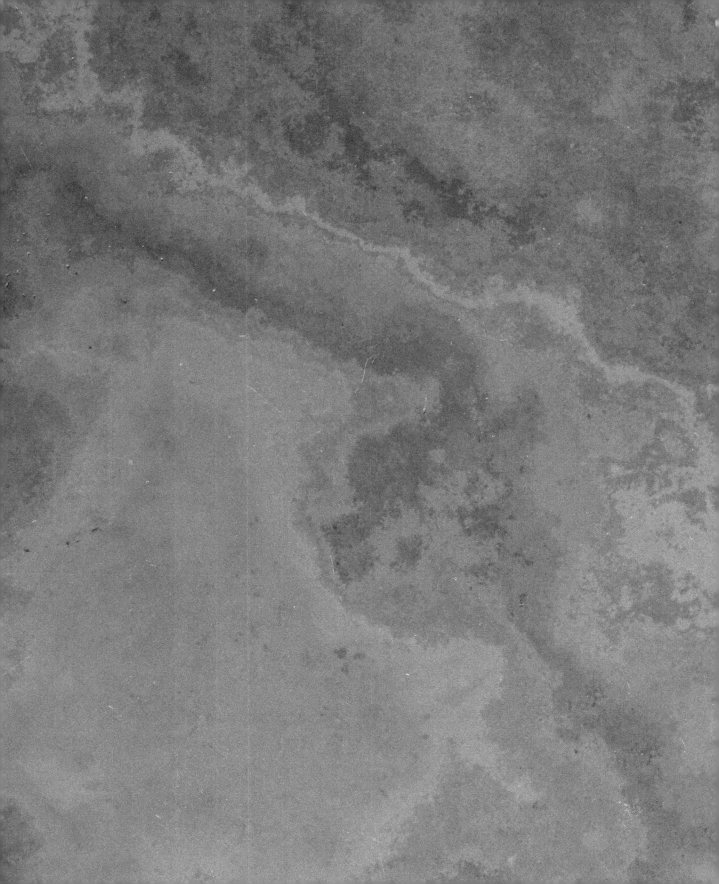

Rustic Roots, page 49

LARGE BOARDS

NEW YEAR'S EVE

SERVES 8

While there is plenty of charcuterie on offer here, the showstopping element of this board comes in the form of raclette. Deriving from the French word meaning "to scrape," it involves melting the creamy, nutty raclette cheese, then pouring it over potatoes. It's a popular New Year's Eve tradition in the Swiss Alps, Austria, and Germany, and we've re-created it here so you can put on a show for your guests, who are sure to ooh and aah as they enjoy cheesy potatoes with pieces of salty prosciutto, salami, and pickled goodies.

2½ pounds fingerling potatoes

1 tablespoon butter

Sea salt

Freshly ground black pepper

10 ounces prosciutto, thinly sliced

10 ounces salami, thinly sliced

1 (16-ounce) jar pickled pearl onions, drained

1 (13.5-ounce) jar cornichons, drained

12 ounces raclette, sliced ¼-inch thick

You will need: a large board, 3 small forks, 2 small bowls, a small spoon, a serving spoon, a fork and small plate for each guest

1. Place the potatoes in a medium saucepan, cover with water, and bring to a boil over high heat. Boil the potatoes until they're fork-tender, about 25 minutes. Drain them and transfer to a large bowl. Toss to coat with the butter, and season with salt and pepper. Place the potatoes directly in the center of the board and smash each one with a fork. Pile them together with a serving spoon next to the pile.

2. Arrange the slices of prosciutto in the top left corner of the board, with a small fork beside them.

3. Arrange the slices of salami to the right of the prosciutto with another small fork.

4. Put the pickled pearl onions in a small bowl and place in the bottom left corner with a small spoon.

5. Heap the cornichons in another small bowl and place in the bottom right corner with a small fork.

6. Heat the slices of raclette in a nonstick saucepan over medium-high heat until fully melted, about 5 minutes. The cheese will have a nutty Swiss cheese aroma when melted.

7. Now for the fun part: Pour the cheese right over the smashed potatoes in front of your guests!

Drink pairing: The richness of the cured meats and raclette is best balanced with a crisp, dry white wine. You can choose your favorite variety, but to keep things regional we recommend a Swiss Chasselas or an Austrian Riesling. Of course, the night wouldn't be complete without some bubbles: pair with champagne or prosecco to bring some post-dinner effervescence and happiness as you ring in the New Year.

SORRENTO SUMMER SOLSTICE

SERVES 8 / PREP TIME: 2 HOURS, PLUS OVERNIGHT TO FERMENT FOCACCIA

Take a trip to the Amalfi Coast with this summery board showcasing a medley of Italian charcuterie: casalingo salami, soppressata, and Parma ham. Casalingo is a mild, garlicky, dry-cured salami, but any dry-cured mild salami will be great. Soppressata is a peppery hard salami from Basilicata, Apulia, and Calabria. Parma ham (also known as prosciutto di Parma) is a dry, salt-cured variety from Parma—any variety of prosciutto can be substituted here.

2 Artisan Focaccias (page 74)

2 cups Fresh Ricotta (page 90)

1 cup Olive Tapenade (page 84)

2 cups Pan-Roasted Garlic Almonds (page 86)

6 ounces taleggio (or brie or fontina)

5 ounces casalingo salami (or any mild salami), thinly sliced

5 ounces soppressata (or pepperoni), sliced

6 ounces Parma ham, sliced

4 ounces fig jam

1 bunch green grapes

1 bunch red grapes

1 pint blackberries

1 pint cherries

16 grissini sticks

6 ounces black pepper crackers

You will need: a large board, a medium bowl, a teaspoon, a cheese knife, 2 small bowls, 2 small spoons

1. Prepare the artisan focaccias, fresh ricotta, olive tapenade, and almonds according to the recipes. The ricotta and almonds can be prepared up to a week ahead of time and the tapenade up to 3 weeks, but the focaccias are best served warm or at room temperature.

2. Put the fresh ricotta in a medium bowl, with a teaspoon. Place it slightly to the right center of the board.

3. Break the taleggio into large pieces and place them in the top left corner of the board with a cheese knife.

4. Place the casalingo salami slices in the bottom left corner. Place the soppressata slices near the bottom right corner. Fold the Parma ham in ruffled layers in the top right corner.

5. Place a heaping cup of tapenade in a small bowl with a small spoon in it and position it above the casalingo salami.

6. Scatter the garlic almonds around the tapenade bowl.

7. Place the fig jam in a small bowl with a small teaspoon sticking out of it, tucked next to the Parma ham on the top right.

8. Trim the grapes into small bunches and group them around the board in any three open spaces. Sprinkle the blackberries over all the piles of grapes across the board to create dimension. Top the grapes and blackberries with the cherries.

9. Tear the focaccias into pieces. Fill in the blank spaces on the board with the focaccia, grissini sticks, and black pepper crackers.

Drink pairing: Rosé pairs beautifully with the delicate cheeses and the lightness of this summery spread. A good option is Spumante Brut Rosé, a fruity and floral Italian variety with a hint of bubbles.

P IS FOR PANCETTA

SERVES 8 / PREP TIME: 30 MINUTES

Rich and salty pancetta takes pride of place in this spread. The Italian cousin of bacon, rather than being smoked, it is made by curing pork belly with salt, pepper, and spices, then rolling it into a tight cylinder. The other blockbuster flavor on this board comes in the form of gorgonzola. While sweet and mild when young, as this cheese ages its taste becomes more intense and its aroma more pungent. Ciabatta bread serves as the ideal vessel to soak up all the flavors, which include crumbly Parmigiano-Reggiano, charred artichoke hearts, and homemade artichoke-garlic chili oil.

1 cup Citrus Aioli
(page 85)

¼ cup Artichoke-Garlic
Chili Oil (page 81)

12 ounces
pancetta, cubed

5 artichokes

3 ounces
Parmigiano-Reggiano
(or parmesan)

Freshly ground
black pepper

7½ ounces gorgonzola
(or any blue cheese)

4 loaves ciabatta

Sea salt

You will need:
a large board, a cheese
knife, a small bowl,
a small spoon

1. Prepare the citrus aioli and artichoke-garlic chili oil according to the recipes. Both can be made up to a week ahead of time.

2. In a medium skillet, sauté the pancetta cubes over medium-high heat until crispy, about 5 minutes. Transfer to a plate and set aside.

3. Prepare the artichokes by cutting off the tops of the bulb, then peeling back and removing the leaves to expose the heart. Cut each heart in half and drizzle 2 tablespoons artichoke-garlic chili oil on each one. In a large, heavy skillet, cook the artichoke hearts over high heat, turning to cook all sides, until they are tender and charred, about 4 minutes. Pile the artichoke hearts in the center of the board.

4. Shave about one-third of the Parmigiano-Reggiano over the artichoke hearts, then scatter the pancetta on top and season with black pepper. Place the rest of the Parmigiano-Reggiano on the top left corner of the board.

5. Place the gorgonzola in the top right area of the board, with a cheese knife set between the two cheeses.

6. Place the citrus aioli in a small bowl with a spoon, and position it in the left corner below the artichoke hearts.

7. Cut the ciabatta loaves in half and drizzle a couple of tablespoons of artichoke-garlic chili oil on the cut faces, then sprinkle with sea salt. Arrange below the artichoke hearts along the bottom of the board.

Drink pairing: Select an Italian dry white wine to balance out the big flavors of this board. A great choice is the white-label La Scolca Gavi dei Gavi. A full-flavored wine that is both crisp and fruity, it is derived from Cortese grapes and produced in the small northern Italian town of Gavi. You could also use an Italian Pinot Grigio.

Preparation tip: To save some time making this board, you can buy a jar of artichoke hearts packed in oil.

THREE KINGS' DAY

SERVES 8

This spread is inspired by our experience in Barcelona one Christmas vacation. Beginning at dusk on January 5, the Spanish celebrate Three Kings' Day with festivities and food—and we walked the city streets eating cones of dry chorizo and jamón along with small baguettes. This board features charcuterie similar to what we ate in Spain, including mini chorizos, jamón serrano, and lomo, a dry-cured pork tenderloin, rubbed with salt and paprika, that melts in the mouth. If you can't find it, Italian lardo will give you a similar mouthfeel. Jamón serrano is a dry-cured ham with salty and nutty undertones. These are matched with a trio of classic Spanish cheeses.

4 (6.5-ounce) packages mini chorizo (we like Palacios)

8 ounces jamón serrano (or prosciutto), thinly sliced

8 ounces lomo (or Italian lardo), sliced

7½ ounces Monte Enebro (or any blue cheese)

8 ounces cabra romero (or any goat cheese)

8 ounces Manchego (or any mild sheep milk cheese)

10 ounces quince paste

1 pint blackberries

2 pears, cored and thinly sliced

2 baguettes, cut into 2-inch slices

You will need: a large board, a small bowl, 3 cheese knives, a small spreading knife, a medium bowl

1. Fill a small bowl with the mini chorizos sticking up ready to grab. Place the bowl in the top right area of the board.

2. Lay the jamón serrano slices along the bottom center of the board. In the top left corner arrange the lomo slices.

3. Below the lomo, place the wedge of Monte Enebro with a cheese knife.

4. Place the cabra romero near the top middle with another cheese knife.

5. Shave about ¼ cup of pieces off the Manchego wedge. Place them with a cheese knife and the remaining Manchego wedge in the top right area near the chorizo.

6. Place the cube of quince paste and a small spreading knife above and to the right of the jamón serrano, near the center of the board.

7. Fill a medium bowl with blackberries and set it near the Monte Enebro. Scatter any remaining berries on the board, around the bowl.

8. Arrange the pear slices in an empty space on the left side of the board.

9. Arrange the baguette slices around the board in a few blank spaces to fill in the gaps.

Drink pairing: Garnacha is a red wine from the northeast of Spain. The raspberry undertones pair beautifully with this board. Alternatively, a strong amber beer such as Spain's Cruzcampo Gran Reserva would make a great match, with its hints of caramel, honey, and citrus.

GERMAN SMOKED CHARCUTERIE

SERVES 8 / PREP TIME: 40 MINUTES

This German-themed arrangement is great for a big crowd ready for a hearty meal. You could prepare it to host game day or any backyard get-together. The sausages are the real showstoppers. Bratwurst is typically made with a blend of mostly pork and some beef, and flavored with spices; it is best slightly charred on the grill. Knackwurst, a thick smoked German sausage made from pork and veal flavored with garlic, is best slowly panfried on the stovetop.

2 cups Pickled Red Onion and Fennel (page 68)

1 pound bratwurst

2 tablespoons olive oil

1 pound knackwurst

16 ounces beer cheese (or pub cheese)

¼ cup yellow mustard

2 sourdough boules or loaves, cut or torn into large chunks

You will need: a large platter, 3 forks, a medium bowl, a spoon, a small bowl, a small spreading knife

1. Prepare the pickled red onion and fennel according to the recipe. This can be made up to 1 week in advance.

2. Preheat a grill to medium-high heat. Grill the bratwurst for 15 minutes, turning to char on all sides, until fully cooked through. Transfer to a cutting board and let rest for 5 minutes. Slice on a 45-degree angle into 1- or 2-inch pieces and arrange along the right center of the board, along with a fork.

3. Heat the oil in a medium skillet over medium-high heat. Add the knackwurst and cook for 15 minutes, turning to char on all sides, until golden brown and crispy. Transfer to a cutting board and let rest for 5 minutes. Slice on a 45-degree angle into 1- or 2-inch pieces and arrange along the left center of the board, along with a fork.

4. Fill a medium bowl with the beer cheese and place it in the center of the board, between the two varieties of wurst. Place a spoon in the bowl.

5. Fill a small bowl with the pickled red onion and fennel. Place it just below and to the left of the beer cheese, with a fork.

6. Put the mustard in a small bowl and place it in the top right of the board with a small spreading knife.

7. Place the sourdough chunks around the outer edges all around the board.

Drink pairing: Try Weihenstephaner Pilsner, a light, crisp, clear beer that has an earthy hint of hops and a slightly malty flavor; it is produced in the oldest brewery in Germany. You can mix this up with a Hefeweizen or Weissbier, wheat beers that have a mild but full-bodied quality and a spicy clove flavor.

MOROCCAN MEZZE

SERVES 8 / PREP TIME: 35 MINUTES

This arrangement is a simple twist on khlea, the traditional preserved meat of Morocco. It's made from beef that is cut into strips, marinated with spices, and dried in the sun before being cooked and cooled. You can imitate it here with store-bought jerky and a sprinkle of Moroccan spices.

3 cups Goat Cheese Hummus (page 91)

2 cups Moroccan Spiced Chickpeas (page 63)

Extra-virgin olive oil

2 teaspoons Moroccan spice blend (see page 63)

8 ounces beef jerky (preferably peppered)

8 ounces turkey jerky (preferably cured)

8 flatbreads

½ cup (1 stick) unsalted butter

1 garlic clove, finely grated

¼ cup chopped fresh parsley

16 dates (preferably Medjool)

You will need: a large board, a medium bowl, a teaspoon, a small bowl

1. Prepare the goat cheese hummus and Moroccan spiced chickpeas according to the recipes. The hummus can be made up to a month ahead of time, but the chickpeas are best served fresh, unless you recrisp them in a pan.

2. Place the hummus in a medium bowl and drizzle with extra-virgin olive oil and a sprinkle of the Moroccan spice blend. Put the bowl of hummus in the center of the board with a teaspoon next to it.

3. Place the Moroccan spiced chickpeas in a small bowl above and slightly to the right of the hummus bowl.

4. Arrange the beef jerky and turkey jerky in the top left corner of the board, and sprinkle them with the remaining spice blend.

5. Preheat the oven to 350°F. Place the flatbreads on a rimmed baking sheet. In a skillet, melt the butter over high heat. Add the garlic and cook, stirring, for 5 minutes, until the butter has browned slightly. Brush the garlic butter evenly over the flatbreads and evenly sprinkle the chopped parsley on top. Toast in the oven for 7 to 10 minutes, until the edges are golden. Cut into pieces and place them surrounding the hummus bowl.

6. Place the dates in the bottom right corner.

Drink pairing: Serve with mint green tea and a garnish of fresh mint leaves. Or try a Moroccan spritzer: Combine 1 ounce Cointreau, 1 ounce gin, and 1 ounce mandarin liqueur in a cocktail shaker with some ice, shake, and strain into a chilled tall Collins glass. Finish with ginger beer and a garnish of orange slices and mint leaves.

Preparation tip: If you don't have any Moroccan spice mix, a combo of equal parts garlic powder, smoked paprika, and ground cumin will do the trick.

RUSTIC ROOTS

SERVES 8 / PREP TIME: 2 HOURS, 12 MINUTES, PLUS OVERNIGHT TO BRINE

This versatile arrangement with a vegetable theme can be used for so many occasions. It's a great opportunity to invite friends over for a garden luncheon, a work meeting, or a baby shower or potluck. The crispy cauliflower and spicy dilly beans are great on their own or dipped in the creamy herb yogurt sauce.

1 pint Spicy Dilly Beans (page 61)

4 cups Pan-Roasted Garlic Almonds (page 86)

4 cups Creamy Herb Yogurt Sauce (page 95)

3 cups Crispy Cauliflower (page 67)

1 pound rainbow carrots, peeled and cut into 3- to 4-inch sticks

2 bunches small red radishes

5 ounces salami, sliced

5 ounces speck, sliced

2 cups plantain chips

1 bag tricolored root vegetable chips

You will need:

a large board, a jar or tall medium bowl, a small bowl, a medium bowl, a small spoon, small tongs

1. Prepare the dilly beans, pan-roasted garlic almonds, creamy herb yogurt sauce, and crispy cauliflower according to the recipes. The dilly beans can be made up to 3 months in advance, and the almonds and yogurt sauce a week in advance, but the cauliflower is best made fresh and served warm or at room temperature.

2. Stand the dilly beans upright in a jar or medium bowl with high sides and place it in the bottom right corner of the board.

3. Place the pan-roasted garlic almonds in a small bowl and position it in the bottom left area.

4. Place the creamy herb yogurt sauce in a medium bowl with a small spoon and position it in the upper left area.

5. Scatter the crispy cauliflower florets near the center of the board, cascading down to the bottom.

6. Arrange the rainbow carrots right below the herb yogurt sauce.

7. Place the bunches of radishes to the right of the sauce.

8. Arrange the salami and speck slices in the top right corner, with tongs.

9. Pile the plantain chips in the blank space below the charcuterie.

10. Scatter the tricolored root vegetable chips around the edges, filling in any blank spaces.

Drink pairing: Pinot Grigio pairs well with a light arrangement such as this. The white wine is light and dry, with an almost lemony note, complementing the pickled, raw, and roasted vegetables. It also complements the creamy dip, which has hints of fresh lemon. For a nonalcoholic beverage, a fresh-squeezed mint lemonade would be perfect.

Ingredient tip: To make this board dairy-free, you can substitute bean or pea puree, hummus, or guacamole for the yogurt sauce.

SPANISH SEABOARD

SERVES 8 / PREP TIME: 35 MINUTES, PLUS 3 HOURS TO CHILL

This arrangement brings the flavors of Spain's Mediterranean coast to your home. While the octopus and shrimp may not be charcuterie in the strictest sense, they are a common sight on many a tapas plate in the country (and on antipasto platters across the sea in Italy). Charring the octopus and sautéing the shrimp really elevates their natural flavors. They are paired with the humble Mahón, a smooth, buttery cow milk cheese from the island of Menorca. Pale yellow in color, it has a nutty and fruity aroma. Completing the board are pickled hot peppers, freshly roasted tomatoes and crispy potatoes, and homemade chimichurri.

1½ cups Chimichurri (page 82)

12 Roasted Vine Campari Tomatoes (page 66)

1½ pounds Yukon Gold potatoes, quartered

¼ cup plus 2 tablespoons extra-virgin olive oil, divided

1 teaspoon sea salt, plus more to season

Freshly ground black pepper

1 pound octopus tentacles

½ cup (1 stick) unsalted butter

5 garlic cloves, peeled

1 pound large shrimp, peeled and deveined

10 ounces Mahón (or any mild cow milk cheese)

1 (12-ounce) jar pickled hot peppers, drained

You will need: a large board, a small bowl, a small spoon, a medium bowl, a cheese knife

1. Prepare the chimichurri and roasted tomatoes according to the recipes. The chimichurri can be made up to a week in advance, but the tomatoes are best made fresh and served warm or at room temperature.

2. Preheat the oven to 375°F. Place the potatoes on a rimmed baking sheet and drizzle with ¼ cup of olive oil, 1 teaspoon of sea salt, and a few grinds of black pepper. Roast for 40 minutes, until the potatoes are crispy, golden brown, and fork-tender. Place the crispy potatoes in the top right corner area of the board and season with sea salt and pepper.

3. Preheat a grill or a heavy skillet to high heat. Char the octopus tentacles for 3 to 4 minutes, turning once. Slice into ½-inch pieces and place on the top left side of the board. Drizzle with the remaining 2 tablespoons of olive oil and some sea salt.

4. Spoon some chimichurri over the octopus. Put the rest in a small bowl with a small spoon, below the octopus.

5. Heat the butter and garlic in a large skillet over medium-high heat. Sauté the shrimp in the garlic butter, turning once halfway through, until fully pink, about 5 minutes. Use a slotted spoon to transfer the shrimp to a medium bowl and place in the center of the board.

6. Place the roasted tomatoes in the bottom left corner.

7. Place the Mahón cheese in the bottom right area of the board, with a cheese knife.

8. Place the pickled hot peppers in the middle right area.

Drink pairing: Bodegas Muga Seleccion Especial Reserva Rioja is a Spanish red wine that complements many varieties of seafood, but especially the octopus and shrimp here. It is berry-scented and barrel-aged, which creates a rich, full-bodied wine that can stand up to the bold flavors of this arrangement.

Preparation tip: To take this spread to the next level, you can braise the octopus in a rich and aromatic broth. In a stockpot, simmer 1 cup (2 sticks) unsalted butter, 4 cups dry white wine, 6 peeled garlic cloves, and 1 cup seafood (or chicken) broth. Place 1 to 2 pounds uncooked octopus tentacles (thawed if frozen) into the stockpot and simmer for 60 to 75 minutes, until firm. Transfer to a colander and let cool for 5 minutes, then peel off the skin by rubbing the tentacles with paper towels. Refrigerate in a covered container for up to 2 days, then char as directed on the day of.

GOLDEN CELEBRATION

SERVES 8

This decidedly decadent board features salami flavored with one of the world's great gastronomic pleasures: truffles (known as *tartufo* in Italy). While you can use another salami in a pinch, it's worth buying this variety in a store or online to savor its delicately earthy infusion of hand-harvested Italian truffles. The salami is complemented by the sweet, earthy tones of baked Camembert, a creamy and buttery cow milk cheese from the Normandy region of France. Baguette serves as a neutral vessel for the ingredients, alongside sweet notes in the form of chocolate babka, fresh figs, Bosc pears, and white currants.

2 (8-ounce) wheels Camembert

1 cup caramel sauce

1 cup roasted pecans

Sea salt

5½ ounces truffle salami (we like Creminelli Tartufo Salami), thinly sliced

4 Bosc pears, cored and sliced

8 fresh figs, cut in half

1 pint fresh white currants (or Rainier cherries)

1 chocolate babka

1 baguette

You will need: a large board, a bread knife

1. Preheat the oven to 350°F. Line a rimmed baking sheet with parchment paper and place the two wheels of Camembert cheese on it. Bake for about 20 minutes, until the cheese is soft and melty in the center. Remove and transfer to the center of your serving board.

2. Gently warm the caramel sauce in a small saucepan just until it's runny, then spoon it over the cheese. Top with a heaping pile of roasted pecans and garnish with a pinch of sea salt.

3. Place the salami slices near the right bottom of the board.

4. Arrange the pear slices on the right side of the board, from top to bottom.

5. Scatter the fig halves around the pears and salami.

6. Place the white currants above the salami.

7. Slice half the chocolate babka, and place the slices and the remaining loaf in the top left corner of the board. Place a bread knife next to the loaf.

8. Tear the baguette into large pieces and place them around the bottom left corner.

Drink pairing: For an equally decadent refreshment, try a soixante-quinze (sometimes called a French 75). This celebratory cocktail pairs beautifully with the caramel, sweet, and nutty notes of the arrangement. Combine 2 ounces champagne, 1 ounce gin, ½ ounce fresh lemon juice, 1 tablespoon simple syrup, and some ice in a shaker. Shake vigorously and strain into an iced champagne glass. Top up with more champagne and garnish with a lemon peel.

AN ITALIAN DATE

SERVES 8

Every element of this arrangement pays homage to the rich culinary culture of Italy. First is salami picante, a spicy charcuterie originating in Calabria that is flavored with chiles and paprika. Accompanying it is speck, a salted dry-cured ham that is aged and smoked. These both work wonderfully with the nutty pecorino cheese. Try to find true pecorino from Tuscany for the fullest flavor. For an even more dynamic flavor combo, drizzle some honey on a pairing of salami and pecorino.

5½ ounces speck, thinly sliced

10 ounces salami picante

8 ounces pecorino, sliced

¼ cup honey

2 (6-ounce) fresh mozzarella balls

2 tablespoons chili oil

Sea salt

Freshly ground black pepper

1 (12-inch) Neapolitan-style flatbread, pizza crust, or focaccia

1½ cups arugula

Extra-virgin olive oil for drizzling

You will need: a large board, a small knife, a small jar or dish, a honey wand or spoon, 2 cheese knives

1. Place the sliced speck in the top left area of a large board.

2. Slice half the salami picante and place the slices and remaining large piece in the top center of the board with a small knife, next to the speck.

3. Place the slices of pecorino below the salami.

4. Put the honey in a small jar with a honey wand or spoon and place it to the right of the pecorino.

5. Place the mozzarella balls on the bottom right area of the board. Drizzle the cheese with the chili oil and season with sea salt and pepper. Place two cheese knives next to it.

6. Cut the flatbread into 2-by-5-inch rectangles and layer them to the left of the mozzarella along the bottom of the board. Top with the arugula and a drizzle of olive oil.

Drink pairing: Vermentino di Gallura is an Italian white wine made on the island of Sardinia, where the grapes love the sea. This crisp wine showcases mineral and saline characteristics that bring out the flavors of charcuterie. We also recommend offering a cappuccino or espresso to accompany this board. It's the Italian way, day or night.

A NIGHT IN

This spread has a little something for everyone: salty treats, a medley of cheeses, and a full spectrum of berries and fruits. The vibrant colors are the first thing your guests will notice about this board, with two types of grapes, raspberries, and dried apricots among the meats and cheeses. There is Tuscan salami, which is flavored with garlic and lardo, and a spicy salami to add some kick to the board. The smoked gouda provides a strong smoky flavor, while the Dubliner is a slightly sharp yet creamy and mildly sweet Irish cheese. Offering some crunch and contrast are our pan-roasted garlic almonds infused with lemon and thyme. All together it makes for a wonderfully varied spread to entertain guests.

2 cups Pan-Roasted
Garlic Almonds
(page 86)

4 ounces Jarlsberg

4 ounces smoked Gouda

4 ounces Dubliner

5 ounces salami,
thinly sliced

5 ounces Tuscan salami,
thinly sliced

5 ounces spicy salami,
thinly sliced

1 bunch red grapes

1 bunch green grapes

1 pint raspberries

1 cup dried apricots

1 traditional
baguette, sliced

1 sourdough
baguette, sliced

You will need: a large
board, 2 cheese knives, a
small bowl, a large bowl

1. Prepare the pan-roasted garlic almonds according to the recipe. These can be made up to a week ahead of time.

2. Cut half of the Jarlsberg wedge into small pieces. Place the rest of the wedge in the top left corner of the board with a cheese knife, and surround it with the smaller pieces.

3. Place the Gouda in the bottom right area with a cheese knife.

4. Crumble the Dubliner into bite-size pieces, and pile them in the bottom left area of the board.

5. Place the slices of regular salami and Tuscan salami above the Gouda, in the middle to right side of the board. Place the slices of spicy salami in the bottom middle area of the board.

6. Trim the red and green grapes into small bunches and stack them in the center of the board, creating some height. Cascade some down either side of the board, filling in a few gaps. Sprinkle the raspberries over the grapes.

7. Tuck the dried apricots into the bottom right corner.

8. Place a small bowl of almonds on the left side, near some bunches of grapes.

9. Place a few slices of baguette in any blank spaces, and offer the extra in a large bowl on the side.

Drink pairing: For a fittingly fun beverage, make a cara cara mojito, a sweet, citrusy, and herbal cocktail with just the right amount of bubbles. In a tall Collins glass, muddle 1½ ounces white rum, 1 mint sprig, and ½ ounce fresh lime juice. Add 1 ounce fresh cara cara orange juice (or regular orange juice), ½ ounce simple syrup, soda, and ice, and stir.

DOLCE MILAN

SERVES 8 / PREP TIME: 35 MINUTES

This board draws inspiration from the prized culinary emblems of Milan and the surrounding Lombardy region. There is traditional Milano salami, a delicious dry-cured variety that is pink, dotted with fat, and flavored with spices. Another highlight is stracchino, a soft and creamy cow milk cheese popular in Lombardy that offsets the savory and sweet flavors of this arrangement. We've also included panettone, a sweet bread from Milan that is traditionally served at Christmas but is now popular year-round. It's buttery and rich, with a light and airy texture—as if brioche and cotton candy had a baby. The spread is artfully completed with monochromatic fruits, Meyer lemon marmalade, and confectioners' sugar.

1 cup Meyer Lemon Marmalade (page 94)

7 ounces stracchino (or ricotta)

5½ ounces Milano salami, thinly sliced

12 ounces Iberian shoulder ham (or any mild ham), thinly sliced

1 loaf panettone (or fruit bread or brioche)

½ cup (1 stick) unsalted butter, melted

Confectioners' sugar, for dusting

1 pint fresh figs, halved

1 pint blackberries

1 pint blueberries

You will need: a large platter, 2 small bowls, 2 small spoons

1. Prepare the Meyer lemon marmalade according to the recipe. This can be made up to 2 months in advance.

2. Place the stracchino cheese in a small bowl with a spoon next to it, in the top left area but away from the edge of the board.

3. Place the slices of Milano salami in the top right, along the edge of the board, near the stracchino.

4. Arrange the slices of Iberian ham in the middle right side of the board.

5. Preheat the oven to 375°F. Slice the panettone, place it on a rimmed baking sheet, and lightly brush the slices on both sides with the melted butter. Toast in the oven for 3 to 5 minutes, until slightly golden and toasted at the edges. Arrange the slices in the center of the board, shingling from left to right. Dust with confectioners' sugar.

6. Place the Meyer lemon marmalade in a small bowl or jar in the bottom right corner of the board, with a small spoon.

7. Place the fig halves in the bottom left corner.

8. Pile the blackberries with the figs but cascading toward the center of the board.

9. Sprinkle the figs and blackberries with the blueberries.

Drink pairing: A great pairing for this board would be a Lombardian red wine such as Valtellina, which is scented with cherry and rose water. Or you can create a fig and vodka cocktail for your guests. First, make a fig and vanilla simple syrup by combining 1 cup chopped figs, ⅔ cup sugar, 1 cup water, and 1 vanilla bean cut lengthwise and seeded in a small saucepan. Bring to a boil over medium heat and stir, breaking down the figs, then simmer for 5 to 7 minutes, until it's a loose syrup consistency. Strain and chill. Then in a shaker, combine 1½ ounces vodka, ½ ounce fig and vanilla simple syrup, 1 ounce fresh lemon juice, and some ice. Shake well and strain into chilled cocktail glass, top off with soda water, and garnish with a slice of fig.

Pickled Red Onion and Fennel, page 68

CHAPTER 6
PICKLES, BITES, AND BREADS

BRINED CUCUMBER RIBBONS

MAKES 1 QUART / PREP TIME: 10 MINUTES, PLUS 25 MINUTES TO BRINE

Brined cucumbers are a zingy pickled bite that can be eaten soon after they're prepared or stored for up to a week. These pretty cucumber ribbons are introduced on the Sour Then Sweet board (page 38) but would also be a great addition to the Everything Brunch board (page 28). We use English cucumbers because of their length, which yields beautiful long ribbons.

1 cup warm water

⅓ cup distilled white vinegar

2 teaspoons sugar

1 teaspoon sea salt

½ teaspoon ground white pepper

4 English cucumbers

1. In a large measuring cup, combine the warm water, vinegar, sugar, salt, and white pepper.

2. With a vegetable peeler, peel the cucumbers all the way down to the seeds, creating long strands of cucumber ribbons.

3. Divide the ribbons between 2 pint-size jars.

4. Pour the vinegar mixture over the ribbons, making sure they are fully submerged, and screw on the lids.

5. Leave to brine at room temperature for 25 minutes before serving, or refrigerate for up to 1 week.

Variation tip: For a slightly different flavor profile you can use apple cider vinegar or rice vinegar. You can also use this method with other garden vegetables and aromatics, including sliced bell peppers, onions, carrots, beets, and cabbage.

SPICY DILLY BEANS

MAKES 1 QUART / PREP TIME: 30 MINUTES, PLUS OVERNIGHT TO BRINE

One of our childhood favorites, dilly beans are green beans pickled in vinegar seasoned with spices, garlic, and dill seed. They hold special sentimental value as a regular accompaniment to Sunday-night dinners. With plenty of pucker from the vinegar and a nice kick from the cayenne pepper, they balance out the many milder varieties of charcuterie and cheese. To make these, you'll need canning tongs and 2 pint-size canning jars with lids.

4 garlic cloves, peeled

4 teaspoons dill seed

1 teaspoon cayenne pepper

1 pound fresh green beans, trimmed

1 cup distilled white vinegar

1 cup water

2 teaspoons kosher salt

1. Fill a large stockpot halfway with water and bring to a boil over high heat. Place 2 canning jars and their lids in the pot to sanitize them. Carefully remove them with canning tongs and set them aside to dry. Keep the water at a simmer.

2. Divide the garlic cloves, dill seed, and cayenne pepper between the dry jars, then pack each jar tightly with half of the green beans. Trim the beans if necessary to fit them in.

3. In a small saucepan, combine the vinegar, water, and salt, and bring to a simmer over medium-high heat, stirring to dissolve the salt.

4. Pour the warm brine into the jars, submerging the beans, until the brine reaches the tops of the jars. Place the lids and rings on the jars and screw on tightly.

5. Bring the water in the stockpot back up to a boil. Gently place the filled jars in the boiling water and process for 10 minutes. Turn off the heat and carefully remove the jars with canning tongs. Let the jars sit on the counter overnight.

6. The jars can be refrigerated after 24 hours and will keep for up to 3 months.

Serving suggestion: Dilly beans are a great condiment with sandwiches or as an addition to a picnic. They can also be chopped up as a salad topping.

OVEN-DRIED STRAWBERRIES

MAKES 1½ CUPS / PREP TIME: 25 MINUTES / COOK TIME: 3 HOURS

Summer berries picked at their peak are one of nature's greatest treats. And these oven-dried strawberries take them to a whole new level. While they take a bit of time to dehydrate, you need only two ingredients, and there is minimal prep work required before slowly drying them in the oven. The method concentrates the berries' natural flavor, leaving you with a natural fruit snack that's slightly chewy and wonderfully sweet. Raw sugar is also known as turbinado or Demerara sugar, and has a touch of molasses.

1 pound fresh
strawberries, sliced

2 tablespoons raw sugar

Nonstick cooking spray

1. In a large bowl, combine the sliced berries with the raw sugar and toss to coat. Let sit for 25 minutes.

2. Preheat the oven to 200°F.

3. Line a rimmed baking sheet with parchment paper, and spray the paper with nonstick cooking spray.

4. Strain the strawberries but reserve the liquid to use as a syrup. Spread out the strawberries in a single layer on the prepared baking sheet.

5. Bake for 30 minutes, then rotate the baking sheet. Continue to bake, turning the baking sheet every 30 minutes. After 1½ hours, turn the strawberries over and continue the drying process, turning the baking sheet every 30 minutes. Bake for up to 3 hours, until they have darkened in color and are dry around the edges.

6. Cool and store in an airtight container for up to 2 weeks.

Ingredient tip: You can oven-dry any fresh strawberries, even those that are slightly past their prime. If you're making these in summer, get fresh berries at your local farmers' market for maximum flavor.

MOROCCAN SPICED CHICKPEAS

MAKES ABOUT 3 CUPS / PREP TIME: 10 MINUTES / COOK TIME: 15 MINUTES

We can't say enough about these toasty chickpeas. You will be surprised at how satisfying they are, and we know you will come back to this recipe again and again. Better still, they make a healthy, gluten-free, vegan alternative to snack foods like chips. They also are a great topping on salads for that crunchy bite, just like a crouton. The spice blend is packed with flavor and can be used on meats as well as the chickpeas. Make some extra and set it aside, because it's a great spice blend to have on hand. So great, in fact, that we use it in our Moroccan Mezze board (page 48).

For the Moroccan
spice blend
5 teaspoons
ground nutmeg

5 teaspoons
ground cumin

5 teaspoons
ground coriander

3 teaspoons
smoked paprika

2½ teaspoons
ground ginger

2½ teaspoons
ground allspice

1½ teaspoons
ground cinnamon

1 teaspoon
cayenne pepper

¼ cup sea salt or pink
Himalayan salt

For the chickpeas
2 tablespoons
extra-virgin olive oil

2 (16-ounce) cans
chickpeas, rinsed,
drained, and patted dry

Sea salt

To make the Moroccan spice blend

1. Combine all the ingredients in a small mixing bowl and mix well with a spoon, then transfer to a jar and cover tightly. Store at room temperature for up to 6 months.

To make the chickpeas

2. Heat the olive oil in a large skillet over medium-high heat. Add the chickpeas and sprinkle with 1 tablespoon of the spice blend.

3. Roll the pan around over the heat, tossing to coat the chickpeas. Continue to toast for about 15 minutes, until the chickpeas are crispy.

4. Season with more sea salt, if desired, and serve.

5. Store leftovers in an airtight container at room temperature for a few days; they will require a quick toss in a hot skillet to bring back the crispness.

ROSEMARY-LEMON CASTELVETRANO OLIVES

MAKES ABOUT 4 CUPS / PREP TIME: 10 MINUTES, PLUS 1 HOUR TO BRINE

Castelvetrano olives are the mildest, smoothest, and most buttery of all the green olives. They aren't packed in a super salty brine, so they retain a ton of their natural flavors. You can find them with their pits intact or pitted. For this recipe either is great, but we prefer the pits intact as part of the experience when eating them. You can really focus on the hints of rosemary, lemon, olive oil, and garlic here.

1 (20-ounce) jar Castelvetrano olives, drained

½ cup extra-virgin olive oil

5 garlic cloves, thinly sliced

4 rosemary sprigs, cut in half

1 lemon

1. In a large bowl, toss the olives with the olive oil.

2. Add the garlic slices and rosemary sprigs.

3. With a vegetable peeler, peel large strips of lemon peel into the bowl. Cut the lemon in half and squeeze all the juice into the bowl.

4. Toss everything together, cover, and let rest at room temperature for at least 1 hour before serving.

5. Store in an airtight container in the refrigerator for up to 1 week.

APRICOT-CHIPOTLE GUMMIES

MAKES 64 (1-INCH) SQUARES / PREP TIME: 5 MINUTES, PLUS 3 HOURS TO CHILL / COOK TIME: 15 MINUTES

These apricot-chipotle gummies are candy for adults. They are sweet but with a hit of heat, and they have the most amazing texture. Making gummy candy is quite easy to do, and you need just a few ingredients. The recipe can be made with any fruit puree you desire. We pair these with fresh apricots, nutty Manchego, and jamón on the Spring in Valencia arrangement (page 30).

2 cups apricot nectar

¼ cup grass-fed gelatin (or 4 packets plain gelatin)

1 teaspoon chipotle puree (from canned chipotle peppers in adobo sauce)

¼ cup honey

1. Pour the apricot nectar into a medium saucepan. Sprinkle the gelatin over the nectar, stir, and let bloom for 5 minutes.

2. Turn the heat to medium-high and whisk until the gelatin completely dissolves, 2 to 3 minutes.

3. Add the chipotle puree and stir well to combine.

4. Add the honey and continue to cook, stirring continuously, until the mixture boils, about 5 minutes.

5. Stir to make sure everything is dissolved and mixed well. Remove the pan from the heat and pour the mixture into a silicone mold or an 8-inch square glass baking pan.

6. Refrigerate for at least 3 hours, or until set. If you aren't using a mold, cut into 1-inch squares. Store in an airtight container in the refrigerator for up to 2 weeks.

ROASTED VINE CAMPARI TOMATOES

SERVES 8 / PREP TIME: 3 MINUTES / COOK TIME: 15 MINUTES

While bundles of vine tomatoes look great on a charcuterie board, by roasting them you enhance their delicious sweetness and acidity while achieving a lightly charred appearance. They burst with flavor and make an impeccable coupling with many varieties of meat and cheeses. You can even spread them onto artisan bread before topping it with your desired accompaniments—or just a pinch of coarse sea salt.

2 pounds on-the-vine Campari tomatoes

2 tablespoons extra-virgin olive oil

Sea salt

Freshly ground black pepper

1. Preheat the oven to 350°F. Line a rimmed baking sheet with parchment paper.

2. Place the whole tomatoes with vines intact in a single layer on the prepared baking sheet.

3. Drizzle the tomatoes with the olive oil and salt liberally. Grind some black pepper over them.

4. Roast for 15 minutes, or until the skins begin to split. Serve warm.

Ingredient tip: You can choose any variety of small, sweet vine tomatoes for this recipe, including cherry or grape tomatoes. Just make sure the vine and tomato bundles stay attached for maximum aesthetic appeal.

CRISPY CAULIFLOWER

SERVES 8 / PREP TIME: 5 MINUTES / COOK TIME: 15 MINUTES

Once cauliflower becomes brown and crispy, it takes on a deep, nutty flavor that's wonderfully suited to ingredients like parmesan, pecorino, sharp white cheddar, and salty Parma ham. This recipe is used in the Rustic Roots board (page 49), but it would make an easy and delightful addition to many of the spreads in this book.

4 tablespoons (½ stick) unsalted butter

3 tablespoons extra-virgin olive oil

Pinch crushed red pepper

5 thyme sprigs

1 head cauliflower, cut into florets

1½ teaspoons sea salt

1. Heat the butter and olive oil in a large skillet over medium-high heat.

2. Add the crushed red pepper, thyme sprigs, and cauliflower florets. Season with the sea salt.

3. Sauté the cauliflower for 10 to 15 minutes, until it's golden brown on the edges. While it cooks, shake the pan occasionally to prevent the florets from burning. Serve warm.

PICKLED RED ONION AND FENNEL

MAKES 1 QUART / PREP TIME: 15 MINUTES, PLUS 25 MINUTES TO BRINE

If you have never tried it, fennel can be very surprising. Its flavor is reminiscent of black licorice, and its texture is very crispy and crunchy. It can be eaten raw, cooked, or pickled. The sharp red onion and licorice-like fennel with honey and apple cider vinegar work so well together. The briny acidity cuts through rich fatty meats like salami and duck confit, as well as buttery cheeses like brie, Wensleydale, burrata, and soft farmer's cheese.

⅔ cup water

½ cup apple cider vinegar

1 tablespoon honey

1 teaspoon sea salt

1 red onion, halved and sliced into paper-thin slices

1 fennel bulb, fronds trimmed, bulb halved and thinly sliced

1. In a small saucepan, combine the water, apple cider vinegar, honey, and salt, and cook over medium heat, stirring, until simmering, then turn off the heat.

2. Place the onion and fennel slices in a quart-size jar. Pour the warm vinegar mixture over the onion and fennel, making sure they are submerged. Let cool, then screw on the lid.

3. Refrigerate for at least 25 minutes before serving, or up to 1 week.

SPANISH TORTILLA

SERVES 8 / PREP TIME: 15 MINUTES / COOK TIME: 35 MINUTES

While walking the streets of Spain, you'll likely pop into a bar and see bite-size pieces of tortilla de patatas on display at the counter. It's a humble dish made of potatoes, onions, and eggs. It takes a little bit of finesse to execute, but with practice becomes an easy technique. The finished tortilla should be rich and hearty, yet soft and smooth, with a golden exterior.

5 tablespoons extra-virgin olive oil, divided

5 Yukon Gold potatoes, peeled and sliced ⅛ inch thick

Sea salt

1 medium yellow onion, thinly sliced

7 large eggs, beaten

1. In a large skillet, heat 3 tablespoons of oil over medium-high heat. Add the potatoes and a pinch of salt. Toss to coat and gently cook, turning the potatoes occasionally, until the potatoes are slightly tender, about 10 minutes. Reserve the skillet.

2. While the potatoes are cooking, heat the remaining 2 tablespoons of oil in a medium skillet over medium-high heat. Add the onion and a pinch of salt and cook, stirring occasionally, until it caramelizes, about 10 minutes.

3. Combine the cooked potatoes and caramelized onion in a large mixing bowl and strain off the oil. Reserve 3 tablespoons. Toss the potatoes and onion with the beaten eggs and a pinch of salt.

4. Heat the reserved 3 tablespoons of oil in the same large skillet over medium-high heat. Add the potato mixture to the pan and spread out into an even layer. Reduce the heat to medium-low. Cook for 7 to 10 minutes, until the bottom forms a golden crust.

5. Get ready to flip the tortilla. Place a plate larger than the pan over the potatoes, hold the pan handle and the plate firmly, and flip. Put the pan down, and carefully yet swiftly slide the tortilla off the plate and back into the pan. Cook for another 5 minutes, or until set.

6. Slide the tortilla out onto a serving plate or board. Let cool for 10 minutes before slicing and serving. Store leftovers, wrapped in plastic wrap, in the refrigerator for up to 1 day. Reheat in a warm oven before serving.

DUCK CONFIT

SERVES 4 / PREP TIME: 3 MINUTES / COOK TIME: 2 HOURS

Duck confit is featured on our South of France board (page 34). It uses a centuries-old French technique to slowly render duck in its own fat, producing a luxurious, rich meat that is slightly salty yet mild. You can reuse the leftover duck fat to fry potatoes, sauté vegetables, or enhance pan sauces.

2 bone-in, skin-on whole duck legs (thigh plus drumstick)

2 tablespoons duck fat

Sea salt

1. Preheat the oven to 350°F.

2. Place the duck legs and duck fat in a small baking pan.

3. Roast in the oven until the meat is very tender, about 2 hours.

4. Transfer the legs to a cutting board and shred the skin and meat off the bones using 2 forks.

5. Mix the skin and meat with the rendered fat remaining in the pan. Season with sea salt.

6. Store the confit in its fat in an airtight container in the refrigerator for up to 3 months.

Serving suggestion: Confit should be served warm. Gently warm it in a saucepan over medium heat for about 10 minutes.

MINI CHAFFLES

MAKES 4 / PREP TIME: 5 MINUTES / COOK TIME: 6 MINUTES

A ketogenic version of waffles that have become increasingly popular in recent times, "chaffles" make a great low-carb substitute for bread—even on a charcuterie board. Made from cheese and eggs, they do not need to be sweetened like regular waffles, and can be topped with all manner of ingredients, including cured meats, avocado, and spreads. We've used mozzarella here, but you can change up the flavor by using your favorite melting cheese.

1 cup shredded mozzarella (preferably freshly shredded)

2 large eggs, beaten

2 tablespoons almond flour

Nonstick cooking spray

1. Preheat a mini waffle iron to medium-high.

2. In a small bowl, combine the shredded mozzarella, eggs, and almond flour. Stir until the batter is well combined.

3. Divide the mixture into four equal portions. Spray the cooking spray on the preheated waffle iron, scoop one portion onto the waffle iron, shut the lid, and cook until crispy. This should take 1 to 2 minutes, but follow your waffle iron instructions. Repeat with the remaining portions.

4. Let cool for 2 to 3 minutes before serving.

Preparation tip: You won't achieve quite the same size, but you can also make these in a classic waffle iron. You can also use the batter to make pancakes in a small skillet.

THYME SHORTBREAD

MAKES 24 PIECES / PREP TIME: 15 MINUTES, PLUS 15 MINUTES TO CHILL / COOK TIME: 25 MINUTES

One of the beautiful things about this crispy, crumbly thyme shortbread is that it is very versatile. It becomes sweeter when paired with the flavors of fruit and marmalades, or it can pick up savory notes when matched with salty meats and cheeses. The buttery sweet flavors melt in your mouth—with a hint of herbal essence.

1 vanilla bean

3 sticks unsalted butter, softened

1 cup sugar

3½ cups all-purpose flour

¼ teaspoon sea salt

Grated zest of 1 lemon

Leaves from 8 thyme sprigs

1. Run the tip of a paring knife down the length of the vanilla bean. Scrape and remove the seeds, and set them aside.

2. In the bowl of an electric stand mixer fitted with the paddle attachment, or in a large mixing bowl with a handheld electric mixer, combine the butter and sugar. Once fully combined, add the vanilla bean seeds and beat into the butter mixture.

3. Turn the mixer to low, add the flour, sea salt, and lemon zest, and beat until fully combined. Add the thyme leaves and mix gently until the dough has fully combined.

4. Scoop all the dough onto a long piece of plastic wrap. Fold the wrap over the dough and use your hands to shape it into a log about 2 inches in diameter. Refrigerate until firm, 15 to 20 minutes.

5. Preheat the oven to 350°F. Line a rimmed baking sheet with parchment paper.

6. Slice the dough into ¼-inch-thick rounds, and arrange them on the prepared baking sheet. Bake until the edges are golden, 20 to 25 minutes. Transfer to a cooling rack to cool.

7. Store in an airtight container at room temperature for up to 1 week.

Ingredient tip: You can make small adaptations to flavor the shortbread differently. Chopped pecans or walnuts, sesame seeds, grated lime zest, and a confectioners' sugar glaze are all great variations.

ARTISAN FOCACCIA

SERVES 8 / PREP TIME: 30 MINUTES, PLUS 8 HOURS TO FERMENT / COOK TIME: 30 MINUTES

A classic Italian bread, focaccia is a favorite accompaniment to antipasto boards across the country. We especially love its wonderful texture—from the slightly crunchy exterior to the crispy edges and airy but chewy interior. Its flavor is enriched by the simplest of ingredients, including sea salt and olive oil.

For the bread

3 cups warm water

1 teaspoon active dry yeast

1 tablespoon molasses

5½ cups all-purpose flour, divided

1 tablespoon sea salt

¾ cup extra-virgin olive oil, divided, plus more for greasing and drizzling

1 teaspoon flaky sea salt, plus more for baking

For the brine

1 teaspoon fine sea salt

⅓ cup warm water

1. In a large bowl, combine the water, yeast, and molasses.

2. Add half of the flour and the sea salt and stir with a wooden spoon for 2 minutes, until all the flour is incorporated and a sticky dough forms.

3. Add ½ cup of olive oil and the remaining flour and stir until a shaggy dough forms.

4. Knead the dough on a lightly floured surface for 5 to 7 minutes. This process will help develop the gluten, creating an elastic dough. When the dough ball springs back when you gently press it, it is ready to ferment.

5. Pour the remaining ¼ cup of olive oil into a 6-quart container with a tight-fitting lid, or a large bowl that you can cover with plastic wrap. Transfer the dough to the container, turn to coat, and cover tightly. Place in the refrigerator to ferment for at least 8 hours or up to 2 days.

6. Preheat the oven to 450°F. Brush a rimmed baking sheet with olive oil.

7. Transfer the focaccia dough to the oiled baking sheet. Using your hands, spread the dough out by stretching and pushing it, reaching the edges of the baking sheet as much as possible.

8. Cover the baking sheet with a kitchen towel and place it in a warm place to rise until it doubles in size. This could take up to 2 hours, depending on the temperature of your kitchen. When the dough is ready, it should be room temperature, spread out on the sheet, and fluffy.

9. To make the brine, stir the sea salt into the warm water. Make a bunch of indentations in the surface of the dough with your fingertips. When the entire top is dimpled, drizzle with the brine.

10. Bake for 15 minutes, then rotate the baking sheet and bake for another 15 minutes, or until the top is uniformly golden brown.

11. Transfer the focaccia to a wire rack to cool, then brush with olive oil. Finish by sprinkling on the flaky sea salt. This is best served warm, but you can wrap it tightly and store at room temperature for up to 2 days.

Ingredient tip: Extra-virgin olive oil is healthier for you and has the fullest flavor and brightest aroma. Choose bottles that are dark green rather than clear glass, as olive oil loses its freshness when exposed to light.

YORKSHIRE PUDDING

MAKES 12 / PREP TIME: 10 MINUTES / COOK TIME: 15 MINUTES

These airy, crispy bites are mesmerizing to watch bake. They rise and pop up like little sunrises. The flavor is eggy, buttery, and toasty. They are traditionally made for an English roast dinner to cut the richness of the beef and potatoes, and are scrumptious when used as a vessel to sop up the au jus. We have showcased ours on the Hunting in Manchester board (page 32) in the same way, to balance out the richness of duck jerky, wild boar salami, drunken goat cheese, and caramelized onion dip.

6 teaspoons avocado oil (or light olive oil)

2 large eggs

⅔ cup all-purpose flour

½ cup whole milk

Pinch sea salt

1. Preheat the oven to 425°F.

2. Drizzle ½ teaspoon of oil into each compartment of a standard muffin tin. Place the pan in the preheated oven for 10 minutes.

3. Combine the eggs, flour, milk, and salt in a blender, and blend until smooth, 15 to 20 seconds.

4. Carefully remove the muffin tin from the oven—the oil will be extremely hot, so use oven mitts. Pour the batter evenly into each compartment and place it back in the oven.

5. Bake until the Yorkshire puddings are puffed up and golden brown, 12 to 15 minutes. Serve warm.

EVERYTHING LAVASH

SERVES 10 / PREP TIME: 15 MINUTES / COOK TIME: 14 MINUTES

You'll be amazed at how quick and easy lavash is to bake, and with so few ingredients. It is essentially an unleavened flatbread that takes on a wonderfully brittle and rustic quality when baked. And it can be topped with all kinds of seasoning, sweet or savory. Keeping with the New York deli–inspired theme for our Everything Brunch board (page 28), we have topped ours with "everything bagel" seasoning.

For the lavash

Nonstick cooking spray

2½ cups
all-purpose flour

1 teaspoon sea salt

⅔ cup water

2 tablespoons unsalted
butter, melted

1 large egg white

Extra-virgin olive oil,
for drizzling

**For the everything
seasoning**

2 tablespoons coarse
mineral salt

1 tablespoon dried
onion flakes

1 teaspoon garlic powder

1 tablespoon
poppy seeds

1 tablespoon
sesame seeds

1. Preheat the oven to 400°F. Line a rimmed baking sheet with parchment paper, and spray the paper with nonstick cooking spray.

2. In the bowl of an electric stand mixer fitted with the paddle attachment, or in a large mixing bowl with a handheld electric mixer, combine the flour, salt, water, melted butter, and egg white. Mix on medium speed for about 2 minutes, until it has fully combined into a sticky dough.

3. Scrape the dough onto a clean floured workspace and knead until a smooth dough forms, 2 to 3 minutes. Cut the dough in half and set one half aside.

4. Use a rolling pin to roll the other half on the floured surface as thin as you can.

5. Loosely roll the dough up onto the rolling pin, and use it to lift the thin sheet, transfer it to the prepared baking sheet, and gently unroll it. Drizzle with olive oil and sprinkle with half of the everything seasoning. Repeat with the second portion of dough.

6. Bake until the bread is golden brown and crispy, 12 to 14 minutes. Store in an airtight container at room temperature for up to 5 days.

Meyer Lemon Marmalade, page 94

CHAPTER 7

CONDIMENTS, NUTS, SPREADS, AND DIPS

CABERNET BALSAMIC REDUCTION

MAKES 1 CUP / PREP TIME: 5 MINUTES / COOK TIME: 20 MINUTES

Knowing how to make a classic wine reduction is a great tool to have in your cooking repertoire. With a flavor profile that is sweet, acidic, and reminiscent of a nicely aged fine wine, this silky, rich sauce complements all kinds of meats, cheeses, and vegetables. We have included it on a few boards, showcasing how versatile it really is. And it can be stored in your refrigerator for up to 3 months, so you can pull it out to accompany arrangements with ease.

1 cup balsamic vinegar

1 cup
Cabernet Sauvignon

2 tablespoons honey

1 tablespoon
unsalted butter, at
room temperature

1. Combine the vinegar, wine, and honey in a medium saucepan. Stir and bring to a simmer over medium heat.

2. Continue cooking and stirring occasionally for about 15 minutes to reduce the sauce. It should become thick and sticky, like molasses.

3. When it has reduced by about half, stir in the butter until it is fully incorporated and emulsified, then take the pan off the heat.

4. Let cool, then store in an airtight glass container in the refrigerator for up to 3 months.

Serving suggestion: This reduction isn't just for savory foods. Try spooning some over roasted fruits and gelato for dessert.

ARTICHOKE-GARLIC CHILI OIL

MAKES 3 CUPS / PREP TIME: 5 MINUTES / COOK TIME: 15 MINUTES

Infused olive oils are like sprinkles on a cake: they add a lovely finishing touch to the final product and take it to a whole new level. Our flavor-packed artichoke-garlic chili oil is so versatile—it can be drizzled over fish, mild cheeses, pizza, pasta, roasted vegetables, or salads. Remember, a little oil will go a long way; you can change the heat level by adding more or less chiles when steeping.

2 cups extra-virgin olive oil

1 (10-ounce) jar artichoke hearts packed in oil, drained and roughly chopped

4 garlic cloves, thinly sliced

1 fresh or dried red chile

Pinch crushed red pepper

Pinch sea salt

1. In a medium saucepan, combine all the ingredients.

2. Heat over medium heat, stirring occasionally, until the oil is just about to simmer, about 15 minutes (you will see little bubbles forming along the bottom of the pan).

3. Turn off the heat and leave everything in the pot to come to room temperature. Store in a glass bottle at room temperature for up to 1 week or in the refrigerator for up to 2 months.

CHIMICHURRI

MAKES 3 CUPS / PREP TIME: 15 MINUTES, PLUS 3 HOURS TO CHILL

Originating in Argentina, chimichurri is a versatile herbal condiment that is traditionally served with steak or sausages, but it can be put on all sorts of cooked meats, seafood, potatoes, and vegetables. Not only is it flavorful and brightly colored, it's nutritionally very good for you. Chimichurri is ideal for using up your garden herbs—you can add oregano, tarragon, chervil, chives, or other herbs to this recipe for different flavor profiles. We showcase this chimichurri on the Spanish Seaboard (page 50) with charred octopus, shrimp, Mahón cheese, and crispy potatoes.

1 shallot

2 garlic cloves, peeled

1 serrano pepper

¼ cup red wine vinegar

2 bunches fresh cilantro, leaves and tender stems finely chopped

1 bunch fresh parsley, leaves and tender stems finely chopped

¾ cup extra-virgin olive oil

1½ teaspoons sea salt

Freshly ground black pepper

1. Mince the shallot, garlic, and serrano pepper together almost into a paste. Place in a small glass bowl, cover with the red wine vinegar, and let sit for 5 minutes.

2. Combine the cilantro and parsley in a large glass bowl.

3. Add the shallot mixture to the cilantro and parsley and mix well. Add the olive oil and season with the sea salt and black pepper.

4. Mix well, cover, and refrigerate for at least 3 hours before serving. Leftovers will keep for up to 1 week.

Preparation tip: To save time, you can also make this recipe in a food processor. Combine all the ingredients and pulse until they're combined and resemble a coarse pesto or salsa. Season with salt and pepper.

MUSTARD GASTRIQUE

MAKES ½ CUP / PREP TIME: 3 MINUTES / COOK TIME: 18 MINUTES

Mustard gastrique is a French sauce with a tangy bite balanced with a sweet finish. Traditionally the base consists of sugar and honey mixed with vinegar, and sometimes it can be finished with berries or fruit purees. We took a savory approach to complement our South of France board (page 34), and finished the simmering sauce with whole-grain mustard. Gastrique is a powerhouse of flavor that pairs well with all manner of charcuterie meats, as well as cheeses such as gorgonzola, Roquefort, or double-cream brie.

¼ cup honey

½ cup champagne vinegar

Pinch sea salt

1½ teaspoons whole-grain mustard

Freshly ground black pepper

1. Heat the honey in a small nonstick pan or skillet over medium-low heat for about 5 minutes, until it turns deep amber.

2. Add the vinegar and salt. Continue to cook, stirring with a wooden spoon, to emulsify the mixture, about 3 minutes. Turn the heat to low and reduce the sauce for about 10 minutes, until it is the consistency of a thin maple syrup.

3. Turn off the heat and stir in the whole-grain mustard and pepper. Serve warm.

4. Store the gastrique in an airtight container in the refrigerator for up to 2 weeks. Simply reheat gently before serving.

Serving suggestion: Gastrique is great drizzled over grilled vegetables and meats. You can change the flavors by using different types of mustards and vinegars.

OLIVE TAPENADE

MAKES 4 CUPS / PREP TIME: 10 MINUTES

Olive tapenade is a simple, savory spread made of finely chopped olives mixed with aromatics. It's a great addition to virtually any charcuterie board. Our favorite version is made with three varieties of olives plus artichoke hearts. You get a little spicy bite from the fresh garlic and pepperoncini and acidity from the banana peppers and vinegar. It's absolutely packed with flavor, and pulled together with rich olive oil. It can be served cold or at room temperature.

10 ounces kalamata olives, pitted

10 ounces Spanish green olives, pitted

6 ounces black olives, pitted

1 (14-ounce) can artichoke hearts, drained

¼ cup pepperoncini peppers, drained

½ cup pickled banana peppers, drained

1 garlic clove, peeled

½ cup extra-virgin olive oil

2 tablespoons red wine vinegar

1 teaspoon freshly ground black pepper

1. In a food processor, pulse all the olives until you achieve a coarse texture. Scoop the mixture into a large bowl.

2. Add the artichoke hearts, pepperoncini, banana peppers, and garlic to the food processor and pulse to about the same coarse texture as the olive mixture. Add this mixture to the bowl with the olives mixture.

3. Pour the olive oil and red wine vinegar over the olive mixture, and fold together with a silicone spatula.

4. Stir in the pepper, taste, and add more if needed.

5. Store in an airtight container in the refrigerator for up to 3 weeks.

CITRUS AIOLI

MAKES 1½ CUPS / PREP TIME: 10 MINUTES

Aioli is like a lighter, cleaner version of mayonnaise, without the chemicals or additives, and is simple to make at home. To create an aioli (or mayonnaise), you use an emulsifying technique, in which a steady stream of oil is broken up and fully incorporated into other ingredients though rigorous whisking or blending. The flavoring comes from garlic, mustard, and lemon. If you find that the aioli is too thick, simply add more lemon juice or a small amount of water to thin it out.

1 garlic clove

¾ cup extra-virgin olive oil

¼ cup avocado oil

3 large egg yolks

1½ tablespoons fresh lemon juice

2 teaspoons Dijon mustard

1 tablespoon grated lemon zest

½ teaspoon sea salt

Freshly ground black pepper

1. Very finely mince the garlic into a paste (use a zester if you have one) and set aside.

2. Combine the oils in a vessel with a spout.

3. In a large bowl, whisk together the egg yolks, lemon juice, and mustard. While whisking vigorously, drizzle in the oil slowly but continuously until the mixture has emulsified. It will become opaque and fluffy, like mayonnaise.

4. Add the garlic paste, lemon zest, sea salt, and a few grinds of black pepper, and serve.

5. Store leftovers in an airtight container in the refrigerator for up to 1 week.

Preparation tip: We've described how to make aioli by hand, the traditional way, but you can also make it in the blender. Remove the center plug from the lid. Combine the egg yolks, lemon juice, and mustard in the blender. Turn the blender on at low speed and very slowly drizzle the oil through the hole in the lid until emulsified.

PAN-ROASTED GARLIC ALMONDS

MAKES 4 CUPS / PREP TIME: 5 MINUTES / COOK TIME: 10 MINUTES

Pan-roasting gives almonds the most amazingly crispy texture. And this recipe is full of flavor: you get a natural saltiness from the sea salt, earthy herbal notes from the thyme, and hints of citrus from the lemon peel. These almonds are a great accompaniment to virtually any of our savory arrangements.

1 lemon

4 cups whole
raw almonds

¼ cup extra-virgin
olive oil

5 garlic cloves, peeled
and lightly smashed

6 thyme sprigs

1 tablespoon sea salt

1 teaspoon freshly
ground black pepper

1. With a vegetable peeler, remove all the yellow peel from the lemon and set it aside. (Juice the lemon for another use.)

2. In a large skillet, combine the almonds and olive oil. Cook over medium heat, tossing to coat, for 2 to 3 minutes.

3. Add the garlic, thyme, and lemon peel. Sprinkle with the salt and pepper.

4. Cook, stirring constantly so the nuts don't burn, until they give off a fragrant, nutty aroma and are crispy, 5 to 8 minutes.

5. Cool for about 5 minutes so they can be handled and eaten warm. Or store in an airtight container at room temperature for up to 1 week.

SPICED CANDIED NUTS

MAKES ABOUT 4 CUPS / PREP TIME: 3 MINUTES / COOK TIME: 5 MINUTES

For us, the smell of roasting sugar, cinnamon, and nuts awakens the nostalgia of walking past street vendors selling aromatic candied nuts every winter. While there is nothing like warm, sweet cinnamon in the winter, this arrangement can be made year-round. Be sure to use unsalted nuts for this recipe.

Nonstick cooking spray

1 cup whole almonds

1 cup pecan halves

1 cup shelled pistachios

1 cup macadamia nuts

1 cup sugar

2 teaspoons ground cinnamon

1 teaspoon ground ginger

½ teaspoon ground nutmeg

Pinch ground cloves

1. Spray a rimmed baking sheet with nonstick cooking spray.

2. Combine all the nuts in a large nonstick skillet. Add the sugar, cinnamon, ginger, nutmeg, and cloves.

3. Turn the heat to medium-high and stir the nut mixture continuously until the sugar begins to liquefy, about 3 minutes. Reduce the heat to medium and continue stirring until the sugar caramelizes to a golden amber color, about 2 more minutes.

4. Pour the nuts onto the prepared baking sheet in a single layer. If necessary, quickly spread them out with a silicone spatula. They will be very hot, so be careful.

5. Let cool. Once cooled, break into small chunks and store in an airtight container at room temperature for up to 3 months.

Serving suggestion: Beyond a charcuterie board, these candied nuts are great on top of salads, sweet rolls, desserts, and ice cream.

PECAN GRANOLA

SERVES 8 / PREP TIME: 15 MINUTES / COOK TIME: 30 MINUTES

This homemade granola will make you think twice about buying store-bought versions ever again. It's a simple two-step process using real ingredients. The granola is nutty, with warmth from cinnamon and honey. It's great all year round on top of yogurt, kefir, roasted fruits, or desserts. We use it on our Cherries and Almonds board (page 24), where it complements fresh cherries and meaty bresaola.

5 cups rolled oats

2 cups pecan halves

1 cup slivered almonds

2½ cups unsweetened flaked coconut

½ cup (1 stick) unsalted butter

½ cup honey

½ cup pure maple syrup

1 teaspoon pure vanilla extract

1½ teaspoons ground cinnamon

1 teaspoon sea salt

1. Preheat the oven to 350°F. Line a rimmed baking sheet with parchment paper.

2. In a large bowl, mix the rolled oats, pecans, almonds, and coconut flakes.

3. In a small saucepan, combine the butter, honey, maple syrup, vanilla, cinnamon, and sea salt. Cook over medium heat, stirring occasionally, until the mixture is bubbling around the edges and an amber syrup has formed, about 5 minutes. Pour the syrup over the oat mixture and toss to coat.

4. Pour the mixture onto the prepared baking sheet and use a silicone spatula to spread it out into an even layer.

5. Bake for 15 minutes, then rotate the pan and stir gently. Bake for another 15 minutes, or until the granola is golden.

6. Cool for 20 minutes before serving. Store in an airtight container at room temperature for up to 1 month.

Variation tip: This recipe can be easily modified by adding your favorite dried fruits and/or nuts.

DATE CARAMEL

MAKES ABOUT 2 CUPS / PREP TIME: 10 MINUTES

Date caramel is a healthy raw alternative to traditional caramel. It's vegan and gluten-free, and the star is the soft, sweet Medjool dates. Nature's candy, dates have a naturally sweet caramel flavor. To bring out that sweetness we add vanilla bean paste, sea salt, and almond milk. If you can't find soft, fresh dates, simply soak drier dates in warm water for about 30 minutes, then drain before processing.

20 Medjool dates (or any variety), pitted

1 teaspoon vanilla bean paste

½ teaspoon sea salt

½ cup unsweetened almond milk

1. In a high-speed blender or food processor, combine all the ingredients. Process until smooth; this may take a minute, so be patient and stir as necessary. You can add more nut milk, if needed, to get the right consistency.

2. Store in an airtight container in the refrigerator for up to 3 days, but it's best served fresh.

Variation tip: Feel free to substitute any nondairy milk of your choice.

FRESH RICOTTA

MAKES 4 CUPS / PREP TIME: 15 MINUTES / COOK TIME: 15 MINUTES

You can serve ricotta with many types of foods: on toast with a drizzle of honey, as a topping for pizza, or to lend creaminess to a simple pasta. The silky, luxurious texture of homemade ricotta will make you reconsider ever buying store-bought versions again. Its mild, creamy flavor makes it an excellent supporting actor to mellow out stronger flavors on a charcuterie spread, as on our Sorrento Summer Solstice board (page 43), where it accompanies dry-cured salamis, Parma ham, olive tapenade, and focaccia. It's best to use cheesecloth to drain the ricotta in this recipe, but a thin, clean kitchen towel can do the trick in a pinch.

8 cups whole milk

2 cups heavy whipping cream

1½ teaspoons sea salt

6 tablespoons distilled white vinegar

1. Line a fine-mesh sieve with cheesecloth and set it over a large bowl. Set aside.

2. In a large stockpot, combine the milk, cream, and salt. Bring to a boil over high heat, then quickly turn down to a simmer.

3. Pour the vinegar into the milk mixture and stir. Turn off the heat and let it sit for about 5 minutes. The whey will separate from the curds.

4. Pour the mixture into the lined sieve and let it drain. This should take about 15 minutes, but you can help it drain faster by moving it around with a big spoon and pushing the watery whey through the cheesecloth. The longer you let the ricotta drain, the drier it will become. If you like it softer, stop draining it sooner.

5. Serve immediately, or store in an airtight container in the refrigerator for up to 1 week.

Variation tip: For garlic ricotta, steep 2 smashed garlic cloves in the milk mixture while you are heating it up in step 2. Remove the garlic before you begin step 4.

GOAT CHEESE HUMMUS

MAKES 5 CUPS / PREP TIME: 10 MINUTES

Originating in the Middle East, hummus is now widely enjoyed throughout the world. While you can easily find it in your local grocery store, nothing beats the flavor of a homemade version, which is simple to make in a food processor or high-speed blender. We like to flavor ours with earthy goat cheese, garlic, and Moroccan spice blend.

2 (16-ounce) cans chickpeas, rinse and drained

1 cup tahini

½ cup extra-virgin olive oil, plus more for drizzling

1½ teaspoons fresh lemon juice

1 garlic clove, chopped

1 teaspoon sea salt

8 ounces goat cheese, divided

Moroccan spice blend (page 63, optional)

1. In a food processor or high-speed blender, combine the chickpeas, tahini, olive oil, lemon juice, garlic, and sea salt. Pulse until smooth. If it remains lumpy, drizzle in a little more olive oil until a puree forms.

2. Add half of the goat cheese and pulse until the mixture is smooth. Use a silicone spatula to scoop it all into a medium bowl.

3. Crumble the remaining goat cheese and use the spatula to fold it into the hummus mixture.

4. To serve, drizzle with olive oil and, if desired, sprinkle with a bit of Moroccan spice blend. Store in a covered container in the refrigerator for up to 1 month.

Serving suggestion: We've paired this recipe with the jerky and flatbread in our Moroccan Mezze board (page 48), but it also makes a lovely dip for vegetable crudités as a healthy snack any time of day.

PANCETTA-ONION JAM

MAKES 1 CUP / PREP TIME: 10 MINUTES / COOK TIME: 30 MINUTES

This sweet and salty jam brings together Italian pancetta, onions, and balsamic vinegar—a trio of flavors that go perfectly with cheese and crackers or artisan breads. The two-step process involves only one pan and a little babysitting as the flavors come together, and it's definitely worth the wait. The flavors are rich and luxurious, and the Italian pancetta takes your average bacon jam to the next level.

1 pound pancetta, cubed

1 medium yellow onion, diced

4 shallots, diced

3 garlic cloves, minced

½ cup packed brown sugar

½ cup pure maple syrup

2 tablespoons balsamic vinegar

2 tablespoons apple cider vinegar

1. In a large skillet or Dutch oven, brown the pancetta over high heat until crispy, 8 to 10 minutes. Use a slotted spoon to transfer to a small bowl. Leave the rendered pancetta fat in the pan.

2. Add the onion and shallots to the pan, and sauté over medium-high heat until they caramelize and turn amber-brown, about 10 minutes.

3. Add the garlic and stir for 2 or 3 minutes, until fragrant. Add the brown sugar, maple syrup, and both vinegars. Stir continuously for 5 minutes.

4. Stir the pancetta and any fat in the bowl back into the pan. Cook until the flavors marry and the mixture comes together into a thick jam, about 5 minutes.

5. Cool to room temperature before serving. Store in a covered jar in the refrigerator for up to 2 weeks.

Ingredient tip: If you can't find pancetta in your grocery store, you can replace it with an uncured bacon or smoky bacon for a similar result.

CARAMELIZED ONION DIP

MAKES ABOUT 4 CUPS / PREP TIME: 10 MINUTES, PLUS 3 HOURS TO CHILL / COOK TIME: 27 MINUTES

There's a lot to savor in this dip with a creamy caramelized onion flavor and an undertone of dry white wine. Making it does require a little patience and attention, but it's well worth it. We use a blend of sweet and sharp onions, then finish it with mild chives to add some brightness back in. Molasses brings out the sweetness of the onions and aids in caramelization.

4 tablespoons (½ stick) unsalted butter

1 tablespoon extra-virgin olive oil

2 medium yellow onions, thinly sliced

1 sweet onion, thinly sliced

1 tablespoon molasses

1½ teaspoons sea salt

¼ cup dry white wine

Freshly ground black pepper

16 ounces (2 cups) sour cream

8 ounces mascarpone

2 tablespoons chopped fresh chives, divided

1. Heat the butter and olive oil in a large skillet over medium-high heat. Add the onions, molasses, and salt. Begin caramelizing the onions, cooking and stirring occasionally, to brown them without burning, about 25 minutes. Lower the heat if the onions seem to be burning.

2. Deglaze the pan by pouring in the wine. Continue to sauté until the liquid has been absorbed and evaporated, about 2 minutes.

3. Turn off the heat and season with pepper. Stir in the sour cream and mascarpone until thoroughly incorporated. Stir in 1 tablespoon of chives.

4. Transfer the dip to an airtight container and refrigerate for at least 3 hours (or up to 1 month).

5. When you are ready to serve, transfer the dip to a serving bowl and garnish with the remaining 1 tablespoon of chives. Store in a covered container in the refrigerator for up to 1 month.

MEYER LEMON MARMALADE

MAKES: 2 CUPS / PREP TIME: 10 MINUTES / COOK TIME: 25 MINUTES

Meyer lemons are sweeter than regular lemons and have a hint of tangerine flavor. They have thinner skin and an orangey-yellow hue, along with an intoxicating smell. To make this quick marmalade, all you'll need is four ingredients, and it'll come together in less than an hour. It is delightful served warm or kept until later.

6 Meyer lemons
(or 4 lemons and
2 clementines)

1 tablespoon
unsalted butter

1 (1.75-ounce) package
fruit pectin

4 cups sugar

1. With a vegetable peeler, peel the lemons in large pieces. Slice each piece of peel into very thin strips. Place in a medium saucepan.

2. Juice the lemons (you should get about 1 cup), strain out the seeds, and add the juice to the pan.

3. Add the butter to the pan. Sprinkle in the pectin and stir. Bring to a boil over high heat, stirring continuously.

4. When the mixture is boiling, add the sugar all at once and return to a full boil while stirring continuously. Turn off the heat and let the marmalade cool slightly, just enough so it's safe to handle.

5. Spoon into a small bowl and serve warm, or ladle the marmalade into jars, cover, and store in the refrigerator for up to 2 months or in the freezer for up to 6 months.

Serving suggestion: This marmalade is also great with scones, biscuits, pancakes, crepes, and sweet rolls.

CREAMY HERB YOGURT SAUCE

MAKES 4 CUPS / PREP TIME: 15 MINUTES / CHILL TIME: 30 MINUTES

Creamy Greek yogurt, garlic, and herbs make this sauce fresh and versatile, and the cucumber adds a refreshing coolness and texture. We use this dip on our Rustic Roots board (page 49), which is filled with colorful vegetables from fresh to pickled, and even roasted crispy cauliflower. This dip is best made ahead of time so the flavors have a chance to come together.

3 cups Greek yogurt

1 small shallot, minced

1 garlic clove, minced

¼ cup finely chopped fresh parsley

¼ cup finely chopped fresh basil

¼ cup finely chopped fresh chives

1 tablespoon finely chopped fresh dill

2 tablespoons extra-virgin olive oil

2 tablespoons champagne vinegar (or white wine vinegar)

1 small cucumber, peeled, seeded, and minced

2 teaspoons sea salt

Freshly ground black pepper

1. In a large bowl, combine the Greek yogurt, shallot, garlic, and chopped herbs and mix well.

2. Stir in the olive oil and vinegar. Mix and stir well until everything is thoroughly combined.

3. Stir in the cucumber, then season with the sea salt and the freshly ground pepper. Taste and season again if needed.

4. Cover and chill for 30 minutes before serving. Store in an airtight container in the refrigerator for up to 1 week.

Serving suggestion: If you're not using this sauce on a charcuterie board, it makes a wonderful topping for grilled meats, seafood, and gyros, or as a dressing for a grain bowl. You can adjust the flavor profile by using whatever herbs you have on hand.

CHARCUTERIE GLOSSARY

CHARCUTERIE TYPE	TASTING NOTES	SUBSTITUTION	BOARD RECIPE(S)
Barolo salami	salami cured in spices and Piedmontese wine	Wine- and-garlic-flavored salami	Afternoon for Two (page 25)
beef jerky	lean beef cut into strips, then cured and dried	beef biltong, khlea, any jerky	Moroccan Mezze (page 48)
bratwurst	seasoned German sausage typically made from pork and veal	apple sausage, kielbasa, Polish sausage	German Smoked Charcuterie (page 47)
bresaola	salted and dry-cured beef with salt and warm spices	lonzino	Cherries and Almonds (page 24), Spring in Valencia (page 30)
casalingo salami	mild salami seasoned with spices, wine, and garlic	mild salami	Sorrento Summer Solstice (page 43)
chorizo	spicy Spanish cured pork sausage flavored with garlic and paprika	spicy salami	Happy Hour Tapas (page 36), Three Kings' Day (page 46)
country ham	salty brined and smoked soft ham	boiled ham, spiral ham	High Tea (page 29)
duck confit	duck rendered in its own fat to produce a rich, slightly salty flavor	pulled pork	South of France (page 34)
duck jerky	duck trimmed of fat, cut into strips, marinated, and dried or smoked	turkey jerky	Hunting in Manchester (page 32)
fennel salami (finocchiona)	bold salami seasoned with fennel seeds and red wine	herb-infused salami	The Sicilian Table (page 35)
Iberian shoulder ham	sweet, nutty, not-too-salty ham	any jamón variety, prosciutto	Dolce Milan (page 56)
jamón	salted and dry-cured pork with a smooth texture and intense, savory taste	prosciutto, jambon de Bayonne	Spring in Valencia (page 30)
jamón ibérico	salted and dry-cured pork made from prized acorn-fed Iberian pigs	any jamón variety, prosciutto	Jamón Experience (page 20)

CHARCUTERIE TYPE	TASTING NOTES	SUBSTITUTION	BOARD RECIPE(S)
jamón serrano	salted and dry-cured pork with nutty undertones made from white pigs	prosciutto, jambon de Bayonne	Three Kings' Day (page 46)
knackwurst	aged and smoked German sausage made from pork and veal with spices	bratwurst, kielbasa, chicken sausage	German Smoked Charcuterie (page 47)
lomo	delicate dry-cured pork tenderloin, rubbed with salt and paprika	lardo	Three Kings' Day (page 46)
Milano salami	pink salami dotted with fat and flavored with spices.	dry-cured salami	Dolce Milan (page 56)
mortadella	mild cold cut of pork lightly infused with spices	mild deli meat or bologna	Kids in Bologna (page 21)
pancetta	pork belly cured with salt, pepper, and spices	uncured bacon or bacon	Summer Berry Fields (page 23), P Is for Pancetta (page 44)
Parma ham (prosciutto di Parma)	slightly salty, nutty ham	any prosciutto	Sorrento Summer Solstice (page 43)
pastrami	smoky, peppery brined and smoked beef brisket	brisket, salted beef	Roman Winter (page 31)
pâté	rich savory paste commonly made of chicken liver	foie gras, tuna salad	Picnic in Paris (page 18)
pickled herring	salted herring brined in a seasoned sweet-sour solution	pickled mackerel	Sour Then Sweet (page 38)
prosciutto	nutty and slightly salty mild pork	jamón, jambon de Bayonne	European Breakfast in Bed (page 19), New Year's Eve (page 42)
prosciutto cotto	strong-flavored ham similar to boiled ham	country ham	Roman Winter (page 31)
salami	sausage made with ground pork and cubes of fat, typically seasoned with garlic, salt, and spices	any dry-cured salami variety such as Varzi, soppressata, picante, Genoa, or chorizo	New Year's Eve (page 42), Rustic Roots (page 49), A Night In (page 54)
salami picante	Calabrian salami flavored with chiles and paprika	pepperoni, chorizo, or any spicy salami variety	Salami Lovers Who Keto (page 22), An Italian Date (page 53)
salami with pistachios	Sicilian salami seasoned with pistachio and lemon zest	regular salami dusted with pistachios	The Sicilian Table (page 35)

CHARCUTERIE TYPE	TASTING NOTES	SUBSTITUTION	BOARD RECIPE(S)
salchichón ibérico	Spanish salami flavored with sea salt and black pepper	any Spanish salami	Happy Hour Tapas (page 36)
saucisson sec	French salami flavored with garlic and black pepper	dry-cured salami	Picnic in Paris (page 18)
smoked salmon	smoky flavor from hot or cold smoke-curing	gravlax	Everything Brunch (page 28)
soppressata	spicy salami typically seasoned with red pepper	pepperoni, salami picante	Sorrento Summer Solstice (page 43)
speck	salted dry-cured ham that is aged and smoked	capicola, prosciutto	Rustic Roots (page 49), An Italian Date (page 53)
spicy salami	salami flavored with chiles and paprika	chorizo, pepperoni, salami picante	A Night In (page 54)
truffle salami (salami al tartufo)	salami infused with the rich, earthy flavor of truffle	salami with truffle oil	Golden Celebration (page 52)
turkey jerky	lean turkey cut into strips, then cured and dried	duck jerky	Moroccan Mezze (page 48)
Tuscan salami	salami flavored with garlic and lardo	mild salami	A Night In (page 54)
whiskey salami	salami with notes of whiskey, garlic, spices, and sea salt	Barolo salami, any dry-cured artisan salami	Salami Lovers Who Keto (page 22)
wild boar salami	dry-cured salami made from wild boar meat, typically mixed with pork and seasonings	bold-flavored salami	Hunting in Manchester (page 32)

MEASUREMENT CONVERSIONS

1 POUND CHEESE = 16 OUNCES, SERVES 11 TO 15 PEOPLE

Volume Equivalents (Liquid)

US STANDARD	US STANDARD (OUNCES)	METRIC (APPROXIMATE)
2 tablespoons	1 fl. oz.	30 mL
¼ cup	2 fl. oz.	60 mL
½ cup	4 fl. oz.	120 mL
1 cup	8 fl. oz.	240 mL
1½ cups	12 fl. oz.	355 mL
2 cups or 1 pint	16 fl. oz.	475 mL
4 cups or 1 quart	32 fl. oz.	1 L
1 gallon	128 fl. oz.	4 L

Oven Temperatures

FAHRENHEIT	CELSIUS (APPROXIMATE)
250°F	120°C
300°F	150°C
325°F	165°C
350°F	180°C
375°F	190°C
400°F	200°C
425°F	220°C
450°F	230°C

Volume Equivalents (Dry)

US STANDARD	METRIC (APPROXIMATE)
⅛ teaspoon	0.5 mL
¼ teaspoon	1 mL
½ teaspoon	2 mL
¾ teaspoon	4 mL
1 teaspoon	5 mL
1 tablespoon	15 mL
¼ cup	59 mL
⅓ cup	79 mL
½ cup	118 mL
⅔ cup	156 mL
¾ cup	177 mL
1 cup	235 mL
2 cups or 1 pint	475 mL
3 cups	700 mL
4 cups or 1 quart	1 L

Weight Equivalents

US STANDARD	METRIC (APPROXIMATE)
½ ounce	15 g
1 ounce	30 g
2 ounces	60 g
4 ounces	115 g
8 ounces	225 g
12 ounces	340 g
16 ounces or 1 pound	455 g

INDEX

ACKNOWLEDGMENTS

We would like to thank our families for their love and support throughout our lives and careers. We both grew up in homes where gathering around the kitchen to cook and eat together was a central part of daily life. This tradition lives on and is something that we cherish. We are also immensely grateful to our clients who have also become friends. Thank you for supporting our business by hiring us along the way. You know who you are—we love you and thank you with all sincerity.

ABOUT THE AUTHORS

Marco Niccoli is an executive chef, UVU Culinary Arts Institute board member, keynote speaker, Food Network competitor, and television chef correspondent for local and national brands. He has produced countless events during his 20-plus years in the industry, from intimate gatherings to massive catered celebrations, and has guest cheffed for a network of clients, including leaders in his home state of Utah, celebrities, and US presidents. He and his wife, Aubrey, are the founders of their own cheffing company, a m. niccoli. You can find them at amniccoli.com and follow Marco on Instagram (@MarcoNiccoli).

Aubrey Niccoli began her private cheffing business at age 24, fresh out of culinary school. However, she has never stopped being a student of her craft and continues to bring her knowledge and passion into the kitchen. During her career, she has cooked for an extensive network of clients spanning professional athletes, musicians, executives, and politicians. She approaches food with an emphasis on health and wellness, both at home with Marco and their children and when creating unique culinary experiences for clients.